THE
Green BOOK
OF
BOUNDARIES

EMERALD EDITION

TIFFANY BUCKNER

© 2021, Tiffany Buckner
The Green Book of Boundaries
www.tiffanybuckner.com
info@anointedfire.com

Published by:
Anointed Fire™ House
www.anointedfirehouse.com

Cover Design by:
Anointed Fire™ House

Author photograph by:
Photo by: Brand You Brand Nu

Edited by:
Jose Juguna

ISBN: 978-1-7354654-5-6

I have tried to recreate events, locales and conversations from my memories of them. In order to maintain their anonymity in some instances, I have changed the names of individuals and places and I may have changed some identifying characteristics and details such as physical properties, occupations and places of residence.

Although the author and publisher have made every effort to ensure that the information in this book was correct at press time, the author and publisher do not assume and hereby disclaim any liability to any party for any loss, damage, or disruption caused by errors or omissions, whether such errors or omissions result from negligence, accident, or any other cause.

Note from the Author

Hey you! Thank you for purchasing the Book of Boundaries (Second edition). Before you proceed any further into this book series, I want to share my heart with you regarding this series. After having ministered to or counseled countless women about boundary-setting, it became apparent that the issues that are ever-so-prevalent in this world are mainly centered around a need for boundaries. I can truly say that more than ninety percent of the people I've coached, counseled or mentored were in dire straits simply because they didn't have any solid or healthy boundaries set in their lives. In truth, most people have never had anyone to teach them how to properly set boundaries. Consequently, our mental institutions and prisons are overflowing with people whose minds have been taken over by the enemy. All the same, school shootings, racism, divorce, rape, abuse and essentially every evil thing on Earth has been thriving as the human race continues to descend into madness. This is why I created the Book of Boundaries!

You'll notice that there are five parts to this series. They are:
1. The Edition
2. **The Emerald Edition** (You are here)
3. The Sapphire Edition
4. The Jasper Edition
5. The Ruby Edition

I chose these names for several reasons, but mainly

because of their colors and what those colors represent. All the same, each of these stones could be found in the ephod of the high priest. "Ye have seen what I did unto the Egyptians, and how I bare you on eagles' wings, and brought you unto myself. Now therefore, if ye will obey my voice indeed, and keep my covenant, then ye shall be a peculiar treasure unto me above all people: for all the earth is mine: And ye shall be unto me a kingdom of priests, and an holy nation. These are the words which thou shalt speak unto the children of Israel" (Exodus 19:4-6). Believers are priests or priestesses of the Most High God, and as such, we should not be in bondage to any person or system that is contrary to our design! This means that these books are all about IDENTITY! They will help you to better understand who you are and give you the confidence needed to embrace your God-given identity! Once you do this, it will be easier for you to appreciate yourself enough to establish boundaries.

Each of these books represent your exodus from one mindset to another one. You won't just learn about boundaries, but you will learn a lot about yourself while reading this series! You will learn about demonology, relationships and how the enemy advances against the minds of God's people by simply using the technology of ignorance! You will go from black to blue, from not knowing to understanding why it is necessary for you to set boundaries, what it looks and feels like to live behind boundaries, and what you stand to gain once you effectively set and enforce boundaries in your life. You will learn about the infamous narcissist and how to rid your life of that evil force once and for all. This is a must-have book for the sane and the insane! It is designed to help you to take back the real estate of your mind that the enemy has stolen from you!

In this series, I also shared some of my personal stories and dreams with you so that you can also witness the exodus that I had to take from being a mess to a living message! I shared these stories so that you can know that it is POSSIBLE for you to completely leave and annihilate one mindset and lifestyle, and wholeheartedly embrace another lifestyle that looks NOTHING like the one you left behind!

Welcome to the Book of Boundaries! Warning: revelation produces a paradigmatic shift, which causes things in your life that shouldn't be there to wither up and fall away. In other words, if you like being broken, bound and miserable, don't go any further because the revelation in this series is potent enough to sober you up! But if you're ready for a change, flip the page!

Sincerely,
Tiffany Buckner

Introduction

The emerald stone is GREEN.

The color green, in this edition, represents renewal; it denotes life, praise and growth. It fsymbolizes the emergence and development of new things, new systems and new beginnings.

In this edition, you will start delving a little more into the spiritual side of empathy versus narcissism. All the same, you will learn about legalities, spiritual principles and spiritual disciplines. And of course, you will learn more about the different types of boundaries and how they have affected you. This edition is designed to prepare you for the major shift that is going to take place in your life as you begin to establish and enforce your new boundaries. This will allow God to renew your heart and your mind; this way, old things can pass away, thus allowing God to do a new thing in your life! In short, this book will give you a realistic view of what your future is going to look like with your new boundaries in place.

TABLE OF CONTENT

Understanding the Heart

Proverbs 4:23: Keep thy heart with all diligence; for out of it are the issues of life.

Luke 6:45: A good man out of the good treasure of his heart bringeth forth that which is good; and an evil man out of the evil treasure of his heart bringeth forth that which is evil: for of the abundance of the heart his mouth speaketh.

The Greek word for "heart" is "kardia," from which we get the word "cardio" and it is translated by Strong's Concordance as "mind, character, inner self, will, intention, center." Of course, we know that when the Bible references the heart of a man, God is not talking about the organ in our body that pumps blood. He's talking about our minds. And the reason this is important is because we are living in a time when most people are completely unfamiliar with the concept of guarding their hearts or they simply do not know what this means. Consequently, narcissism is becoming an epidemic of mass proportions. In truth, I don't think we fully understand just how prevalent narcissism is because most narcissists have never been diagnosed with NPD (Narcissistic Personality Disorder). Let's go deeper than that, Narcissism is becoming normalized in the American culture, so much so that people oftentimes defend narcissists and re-victimize their victims in an attempt to intimidate and silence them. It is no wonder that the majority of rapes go unreported. In truth, the majority of people alive do not understand their makeup. And it is for this reason that they repeatedly open themselves up to people who they should have avoided altogether. For example, are you an introvert, ambivert or extrovert? Understanding these small details about yourself can help you to build and flourish in healthy relationships, but if you don't understand why you get anxiety when someone asks to hang out with you, you are setting yourself up for quite a bit of disappointment. But this isn't all we need to understand about ourselves. First and foremost, consider Genesis 2:7, which reads, "And the LORD God formed man of the dust of the ground, and breathed into his nostrils the breath of life; and man became a living soul." What is a soul? HELP Word Studies defines it this way:

> **5590** psyxḗ (from psyxō, "to breathe, blow" which is the root of the English words "psyche," "psychology") – soul (psyche); a person's distinct identity (unique personhood), i.e. individual personality.

So, man became a distinct identity or psyche. And of course, the word "psyche" is from where we get the words "psychiatry" and "psycho," both of which deals with the mind of a human. So, man became aware, awake and alive. Another word for this is conscious.

The psyche or mind of a man is comprised of three sections, all of which directly correlate to the Tabernacle of Moses. In the Tabernacle of Moses, there were three levels; they were:

- Outer Court
- Inner Court
- Holy of Holies

Hebrews 9:6-10 reads, "Now when these things were thus ordained, the priests went always into the first tabernacle, accomplishing the service of God. But into the second went the high priest alone once every year, not without blood, which he offered for himself, and for the errors of the people: The Holy Ghost this signifying, that the way into the holiest of all was not yet made manifest, while as the first tabernacle was yet standing: Which was a figure for the time then present, in which were offered both gifts and sacrifices, that could not make him that did the service perfect, as pertaining to the conscience; Which stood only in meats and drinks, and divers washings, and carnal ordinances, imposed on them until the time of reformation." Notice that the priests were allowed to go into the first tabernacle, but only the high priest could go into the Holy of Holies. In other words, there were boundaries or limitations for every Levitical priest. As a matter of fact, a king by the name of Uzziah became lifted up in his heart (filled with pride) and illegally entered the sanctuary. Let's look at his story. 2 Chronicles 26:16-21 (ESV) reads, "But when he was strong, he grew proud, to his destruction. For he was unfaithful to the Lord his God and entered the temple of the Lord to burn incense on the altar of incense. But Azariah the priest went in after him, with eighty priests of the Lord who were men of valor, and they withstood King Uzziah and said to him, 'It is not for you,

Uzziah, to burn incense to the Lord, but for the priests, the sons of Aaron, who are consecrated to burn incense. Go out of the sanctuary, for you have done wrong, and it will bring you no honor from the Lord God.' Then Uzziah was angry. Now he had a censer in his hand to burn incense, and when he became angry with the priests, leprosy broke out on his forehead in the presence of the priests in the house of the Lord, by the altar of incense. And Azariah the chief priest and all the priests looked at him, and behold, he was leprous in his forehead! And they rushed him out quickly, and he himself hurried to go out, because the Lord had struck him. And King Uzziah was a leper to the day of his death, and being a leper lived in a separate house, for he was excluded from the house of the Lord. And Jotham his son was over the king's household, governing the people of the land." What happened to Uzziah was clear. He illegally entered into a space that was sacred, and for that, he paid the ultimate price.

Again, this directly relates to our hearts. When God breathed into man, he became a living soul. The soul is comprised of our minds, wills and emotions. The mind has three levels; they are:
- Conscious Mind
- Subconscious Mind
- Unconscious Mind

The conscious mind is the outer courts of the soul. The Outer Courts of the Tabernacle were actually common ground, meaning, any Israelite could enter the Outer Courts, but only the priests could go into the second and third level of the Tabernacle. The conscious mind is the waiting room of the heart. Remember, God told us to keep our hearts; other biblical translations say "Guard your heart." This means to monitor and protect the borders of a thing. Any and everyone, as long as he or she was an Israelite, could walk into the Outer Courts. All the same, just about any and everyone can access our conscious minds, since our conscious deals with:

1. What we are presently aware of (whatever has our attention at any given moment).
2. Information we've received but have not yet accepted as truths or rejected as lies.

So, a random man can walk up to you and say, "The sky is burgundy," and in that moment, he'd be engaging your present awareness or, better yet, your conscious mind. Nevertheless, you won't immediately establish his words to be true until you look up at the sky. If you decide that it looks burgundy-ish, you may say, "Yeah, it kinda does look burgundy." If you look at the sky and it looks blue, you'll immediately reject it as a lie, but in this case, not necessarily a blatant lie.

The second layer or level is the subconscious. This is the proverbial heart of a man; it's the epicenter of the soul. The subconscious is where we store our memories, beliefs and everything that's important to us. When a thought, word or imagination enters the waiting room (conscious), it then has to audition to enter the heart (subconscious). If we believe the information to be true, it enters our subconscious, where it begins to root itself and produce fruits. The fruits of our subconscious are called choices. This is why fornication is more of a heart issue than it is a sensual issue. Fornication is oftentimes the product of a hijacked belief system. For example, if a woman doesn't believe that she's good enough to be with the man she's dating or any man, for this matter, she has what we call low self-esteem. This is nothing but a report that entered her conscious mind and was accepted into her subconscious. Nevertheless, the report doesn't sound like, "You're not good enough for him." It sounds more like, "Look at you. You're not that attractive. Why would anyone want to marry you?" This is what the Bible refers to as one of the darts of the enemy. It's a lie that was fired off into her conscious mind, and there, it will manifest itself as an imagination. This is why the Bible tells us to cast down imaginations and every high thing that exalts itself against the knowledge of God, and bring into captivity every thought to the obedience of Christ. What this means is to label the thought as a lie. For example, when Satan was in Heaven serving as one of God's angels, he was referred to as Lucifer, which means "Light Bearer." Once he betrayed God, the Bible tells us that there was a war in Heaven between Satan and his angels. Do you see what happened? His name changed from Lucifer to Satan, which means adversary. In order Michael to cast Satan out of Heaven, God first had to acknowledge Lucifer for who he was—an adversary or enemy of God. Meaning, judgment took place.

This is what we do with a lie. We must first judge it to be a lie, an attack, a false report or ungodly before we can cast it out of our souls' waiting rooms. Otherwise, it will sit in the waiting room, waiting its turn to once again confront us. Again, the lie in her conscious mind sounds like, "You're unattractive! You're fat! You're not his kind of woman!" If she receives the lie or accepts it as a truth, it will then enter her heart and begin to eat away at her self-esteem. Her agreement with the lies could look like:

1. Her sleeping with the guy. This is her way of trying to convince the guy to stick around. If she can prove herself to be a skilled partner in the bedroom, she believes that she can make up for what she believes she lacks.

2. Her breaking up with the guy. Many women opt to sabotage or end a relationship that they don't feel they're deserving of.

3. Her cheating on the guy. Again, many women will intentionally sabotage a relationship when they don't feel that they're good enough to be in it.

4. Her spending excessive amounts of money on the guy. This overcompensation is her way of paying for what she perceives to be her deficit.

5. Her becoming incredibly insecure. In this, she may question him about any and everything he does, and frequently accuse him of being dishonest with her.

Now, please note that the subconscious can be likened to the Inner Courts of the Tabernacle. Only the priests of God were allowed in this sacred space. Nevertheless, King Uzziah decided that he was the king, so he was good enough to walk into this sacred space and light incense to the Lord. What I'm trying to show you is this—your heart is a sacred space! God told us to not unequally yoke ourselves with unbelievers, but many of us are guilty of disobeying Him in this area. Why? Because we thought that we could change the people who we'd given our hearts to. This is the equivalent of accompanying Uzziah into the Inner Courts. He wasn't sanctified enough to be there; he wasn't called to be there! He was a prideful king who'd desecrated the temple of God! This is similar to what Ahab did when he married Jezebel. He took a woman who was ungodly, unholy and wicked, and he brought her into a sacred space. Consequently, when she came into Israel, she began to do unholy things, including killing off the prophets of God. This is what it looks like when you take something or someone out of the waiting room that should have been cast down and invite that thing or that person into the sacred place that is your heart. And the problem with the majority of believers is that when we do this, we find it difficult to take accountability for our wrongs. For example, some women will refer to their exes as "dogs" because those guys desecrated a sacred space (their hearts), and then, they proceeded to mark them as territory, Nevertheless, if I invite a pack of wolves into my home, and they begin to behave as wolves, they are not the problem. They are doing what they normally do in the wilderness. If I see myself as the victim and cast myself as the victim, I'll likely repeat this behavior again and again. The next time, I'd invite a pack of hyenas into my personal space, and then cast myself as a victim when I find them doing what hyenas do—destroying things and making a lot of noise.

The third level or layer is the unconscious mind. We won't spend too much time on this level because we don't readily have access to our unconscious minds. Thankfully, if we're saved, Satan doesn't have access to this level either. He can, however, build a siege wall around the unconscious of a believer. Before we dive into that message, let's establish this fact—the unconscious mind controls our breathing; it also stores our long term memories and traumas. It is the Most Holy Place of our souls. This is the spirit of a man, and because Satan can't possess the spirit of a believer (we have the Holy Spirit), he has to opt to oppress the soul instead. Nevertheless, once a lie enters the subconscious, it opens a door for the enemy. Once he enters the mind of a man, he then begins to burrow or dig. The goal is to get as close to the unconscious mind as possible; this way, he can build a siege around the unconscious. This rarely happens, but whenever it does, we start witnessing people behaving erratically. In other words, a person whose mind has been hijacked to this point becomes a psycho or, better yet, a psychopath. This simply means that the mind of the person has been captured.

As I mentioned earlier, most people don't understand how they're made, so they don't guard their hearts. Consequently, in just about every country on the face of this planet, there is an overabundance of broken and demonized people, but a shortage of deliverance ministers and therapists. We're taught to do everything but guard our hearts! Because of this, the average believer will experience the narcissist. This demonic personality wears many masks, but its traits are undeniable. Some characteristics of narcissism include:

Frequent Lies and Exaggerations	Both narcissists and gaslighters are prone to frequent lies and exaggerations (about themselves and others), and have the tendency of lifting themselves up by putting others down. While narcissists often strive to make themselves seem superior and "special" by showing off, bragging, taking undeserved credit, and other forms of self-aggrandizement, gaslighters tend to concentrate on making you feel inferior through false accusations, constant criticism, and psychological intimidation.
Rarely Admit Flaws and Are Highly Aggressive When Criticized	Many narcissists and gaslighters have thin skin and can react poorly when called to account for their negative behavior. When challenged, the narcissist is likely to either fight (e.g., temper tantrum, excuse-making, denial, blame, hypersensitivity, etc.) or take flight

	(bolt out the door, avoidance, silent treatment, sulking resentment, or other forms of passive-aggression). The gaslighter nearly always resorts to escalation by doubling or tripling down on their false accusations or coercions, to intimidate or oppress their opponent. Many gaslighters view relationships as inherently competitive rather than collaborative; a zero-sum game where one is either a winner or a loser, on top or at the bottom. "Offense is the best defense" is a mantra for many gaslighters, which also represents their aggressive method of relating to people.
False Image Projection	Both narcissists and gaslighters tend to project false, idealized images of themselves to the world, in order to hide their inner insecurities. Many narcissists like to impress others by making themselves look good externally. This "trophy complex" can exhibit itself physically, romantically, sexually, socially, religiously, financially, materially, professionally, academically, or culturally. The underlying message of this display is:

"I'm better than you!" or "Look at how special I am — I'm worthy of everyone's love, admiration, and acceptance!"

Gaslighters, on the other hand, often create an idealized self-image of being the dominant, suppressive alpha male or female in personal relationships, at the workplace, or in high-profile positions of society (such as politics and media). Many gaslighters like to view themselves falsely as all-powerful and strong, capable of dishing out judgments and penalties at will. Pathological gaslighters often take pride and boost themselves up by marginalizing those whom they perceive as weaker, believing that the meek deserve their downtrodden fate. They attack their victims with direct or subtle cruelty and contempt, gaining sadistic pleasure from these offenses, and betraying a lack of empathy and humanity.

In essence, narcissists want others to worship them, while gaslighters want others to submit to them. In a big way, these external facades become

	pivotal parts of their false identities, replacing the real and insecure self.
Rule Breaking and Boundary Violation	Many narcissists and gaslighters enjoy getting away with violating rules and social norms. Examples of narcissistic trespass include cutting in line, chronic under-tipping, personal space intrusion, borrowing items without returning, using other's properties without asking, disobeying traffic laws, breaking appointments, and negating promises. Examples of gaslighting trespass include direct or subtle marginalizing remarks, public or private shaming and humiliation, sardonic humor and sarcastic comments, internet trolling, angry and hateful speech, and virulent attacks on undesirable individuals and groups. Both narcissist and gaslighter boundary violations presume entitlement, with a narrow, egocentric orientation that oppresses and de-humanizes their victims. In severe cases, this boundary violation pathology may result in illicit and underhanded dealings, financial abuse, sexual harassment, date rape,

	domestic abuse, hate crimes, human rights violations, and other forms of criminality. Many narcissists and gaslighters take pride in their destructive behaviors, as their machinations provide them with a hollow (and desperate) sense of superiority and privilege.
Emotional Invalidation and Coercion	Although narcissists and gaslighters can be (but are not always) physically abusive, for the majority of their victims, emotional suffering is where the damage is most painfully felt. Both narcissists and gaslighters enjoy spreading and arousing negative emotions in order to feel powerful, and keep you insecure and off-balance. They habitually invalidate others' thoughts, feelings, and priorities, showing little remorse for causing people in their lives pain. They often blame their victims for having caused their own victimization ("You wouldn't get yelled at if you weren't so stupid!"). In addition, many narcissists and gaslighters have unpredictable mood swings and are prone to emotional drama — you never know what might

	displease them and set them off. They become upset at any signs of independence and self-affirmation ("Who do you think you are!?"). They turn agitated if you disagree with their views or fail to meet their expectations. As mentioned earlier, they are sensitive to criticism, but quick to judge others. By keeping you down and making you feel inferior, they boost their fragile ego, and feel more reassured about themselves.
Manipulation: The Use or Control of Others as an Extension of Oneself	Both narcissists and gaslighters have a tendency to make decisions for others to suit their own agenda. Narcissists may use their romantic partner, child, family, friend, or colleague to meet unreasonable self-serving needs, fulfill unrealized dreams, or cover-up weaknesses and shortcomings. Narcissists are also fond of using guilt, blame, and victimhood as manipulative devices.

Chart Source: Psychology Today/6 Common Traits of Narcissists and Gaslighters/Preston Ni M.S.B.A.

Again, narcissism is a growing epidemic in this country and all around the world. The medical world calls it narcissism, but in the church, we call it the Jezebel spirit. Let's look at some characteristics of the Jezebel spirit.

1. **Jezebel, in the Bible, was a woman.** But don't run just yet! The Jezebel spirit can be in both men and women! Nevertheless, remember that God gave the husband authority over his wife. Now, this doesn't mean that he can control her; it simply means that he has been entrusted by God to lead his wife and children in the Lord. But get this—it is possible for a woman to have a greater anointing than the man she pairs herself with! The anointing is the blessing or empowerment of God to carry out a certain task. What this means is, if a woman grows impatient and marries a man who has the Jezebel spirit, he is the weaker of the two (emotionally and mentally) in that relationship, even though she's the weakest physically. Consequently, he will use manipulation and every emotional tactic he can conjure up to bait and control her. This is to say that in the Jezebel/Ahab duo, Ahab (the empath) is oftentimes the chosen or anointed one of God. This is the wisest one, nevertheless, the person is being led or controlled by someone who's pretending to be wiser, smarter or more anointed.

2. **Jezebel absolutely has to be in control.** People with this spirit are terrified of losing control over the people in their lives. They use emotional manipulation, intimidation, isolation and a host of other tools to dominate and control another human being. Please note that not all control is dominant

control. Sometimes, the narcissist can be passive and soft-spoken, while the empath is dominant and pushy. When this happens, the passive narcissist will control his or her dominant lover using the tools of manipulation like tears, victimhood and they will even use the people who see them as the "nice ones" in the relationship to bring their lovers back under their control. These types of narcissists are referred to as covert narcissists.

3. **Jezebels cannot and will not accept responsibility for their wrongs.** And if they appear to take responsibility, they will share some of the blame with someone else. Eventually, they'll cast all the blame on the other person.

4. **Jezebel is a compulsive liar.** The reason for this is, most people who are bound by this spirit are often guilty of doing some pretty wicked things to the people in their lives. Because of this, they have to cover up their trails in order to maintain control over these people. They believe that telling the truth would give the other person a measure of power over them, which would then render them powerless. Again, they fear losing control, so because of this, they lie—repeatedly!

5. **Jezebel hates and destroys God's prophets.** Remember, empaths are oftentimes prophets or prophetic individuals. Most of them are extremely prophetic; this is why empaths are super sensitive. You need that level of sensitivity to hear from God.

Nevertheless, Satan knows how you're wired, even when you are not cognizant of this! Therefore, by default, narcissistic people are attracted to empathic people. Another way of saying this is—Jezebel is married to Ahab in the realm of the spirit. Please note that when a narcissist secures a relationship with a prophetic individual, the narcissist cannot and will not love the person. Instead, the narcissistic individual will love the attention, praise, gifts and affirmations that he or she gets from the empath, but it is nearly (if not completely) impossible for a narcissist to love anyone other than himself or herself.

Of course, these are just a few traits of the Jezebel spirit or I can say it this way—these are just a few characteristics of the narcissistic personality. Again, God told us to guard our hearts. This means that everything that enters into the waiting rooms of our conscious should be tested and addressed. If it's a lie, cast it down. If it's a truth, believe it; this is what graduates it from the conscious to the subconscious, where it can then root itself and begin to produce fruit. These fruits act as magnets for more truths; they also act as antibodies, so when a lie comes and sits in the conscious mind, the truths that you have stored in your heart will come forth to address them. For example, if someone said to me, "The Bible is flawed because it was written by man," I know the truth, so their lies, and their logic would not be received by me. Instead, 2 Timothy 3:16-17 would step outside of my subconscious to address this lie. It reads, "All Scripture is breathed out by God and profitable for teaching, for reproof, for correction, and for training in righteousness, that the man of God may be complete, equipped for every good work." In other words, the lie will be slaughtered in the waiting room. Howbeit, if I wasn't someone who studied the Bible, it is possible that I could have accepted that person's flawed logic as my own. Eventually, I'd be sharing the same lies with nothing but a bunch of history lessons and emotional rhetoric to back it.

The point is—we have to understand our makeup in order to protect ourselves from narcissistic/Jezebellic people and any other toxic individuals who would attempt to enter our lives. God told us to guard our hearts, but many of us have failed to do this. In truth, many of us have never been taught to do this. Remember, common people were allowed in the Outer Courts of the Temple, but only the priests of God were allowed into the Inner Court. All the same, only the high priest was allowed into the Most Holy Place. Jesus is our High Priest. If you allow anyone into the space that He is supposed to be occupying, that person will become an idol in your life and will wreak havoc in your life. Your heart is sacred. You don't have the legal right to give it away to anyone. It belongs to God. This is why He'll allow it to become too much of a burden for anyone you hand it to, if that person is not someone He has approved for your life. Yes, He's that good of a Father, even when it doesn't feel like it!

GUARDING YOUR HEART

Recently, I had a dream that I was at some type of camp resort. It was a beautiful place; it looked like something you'd see in a movie. Nevertheless, I wasn't alone. There were a lot of familiar and not-so-familiar faces at the resort, and I understood that we were all there to have our creative abilities judged. It was like an award show type setting. There were many categories that were going to be judged, and there would be one winner for each category. When it was a group's time to be judged, that group would get into a large wooden wagon and the winner would be announced. All the same, we had a beautifully laminated menu with all the categories on it and the names of the people who would be judged in each category.

All of a sudden, the announcer called out for those who were in the beauty pageant, and I tried to move out of the way to let the people get onto the wagon, but somehow, I ended up on the wagon. When I realized I was on the wagon, I said, "I'm not in this category." The truth of the matter is, I didn't feel beautiful at all, nor did I feel worthy to be on that wagon with all of those beautiful people. I reiterated that I wasn't supposed to be on the wagon, but it was as if the people either couldn't hear me; either that, or they were ignoring me. I looked around at the people on the wagon and I could tell that they had been talking negatively about me. They seemed to all be communicating with each other, but they all made it a point to ignore me. That's when the announcer called my name, announcing me as the winner. I was shocked! But before I could respond, my dog woke me up. A few minutes later, I drifted back off to sleep, and I reentered the dream. This time, they were about to judge minstrels. Again, I wasn't supposed to be in that category; I hadn't registered for it, and I'm definitely not a person who is largely into music. I've written a few songs, hired some artists to record those songs, and I've released them on a few outlets like Amazon and iTunes, but that's the extent of it. I haven't chased the world of music, so when they shoved me onto the wagon again to be judged, I tried to tell the announcers that they'd made a mistake. I looked at the menu, and I don't remember seeing my name in that category. I looked around and I was on the wagon with some pretty talented people, many of whom I recognized, and once again, they all ignored me. I felt disconnected from them or, better yet, set apart. Like before, the announcer declared me as the winner. I stood to my feet and tried to protest because I didn't want to further offend the people on the wagon with me, after all, I hadn't registered for those categories, nor did I feel qualified to even be considered. After this, I woke up. What did those dreams mean? In truth, God used those dreams to communicate with me after I'd suffered through a very difficult season. You see, I was dealing with rejection, and not the perception of it, but the reality of it. There are two degrees of rejection, and they are:

1. Perceived

2. Actual

Perceived rejection is oftentimes demonic. It stems from a person dealing, for example, with actual rejection from someone significant. In most cases, this is one or both of that individual's parents. Please note that a parent can be present and still reject a child or cause the child to feel rejected. For example, if the parent is an addict, the parent is abusive or the parent is distant, the child will experience the sting of rejection. This rejection can cause some pretty significant behavioral and/or developmental issues. The child then starts experiencing rejection from his or her peers because of these issues, thus causing rejection to burrow itself deeper and deeper into the child's subconscious. Eventually, the child starts dealing with perceived rejection, and this, if not addressed, will be carried over into adulthood. Perceived rejection is when a person believes that he or she is being rejected by a person or a group of people when this is not true. This is the demonic side of rejection. To the offended party, this is a very real and tangible reality, but the person or people who the individual is offended with are oftentimes unaware of the offended party's beliefs. This then opens the door for the fear of rejection, which is a whole other issue (and spirit) within itself. People suffering with the fear of rejection will oftentimes sabotage relationships anytime they feel rejected, disconnected, or in some cases, too connected to a person. Because they fear being rejected, they try to hold on to some semblance of power and dignity by rejecting people before those people reject them. Howbeit, I was dealing with actual rejection (I won't go into the details). And normally, if a person or a group of people are stand-offish from me, I don't internalize it because I know that anyone who accomplishes any great or small feat in the Earth will have to deal with people who reason within their minds that the individual isn't deserving of the success that he or she has, or they'll reason that they themselves are more deserving of whatever it is that another person has accomplished or been graced with. If you marry a good man, some woman will say in her heart (or aloud) that you don't deserve him. If you start a successful business, someone will say in his or her heart (or aloud) that you are not deserving of that success. If you write a book, someone will opt not to read it because he or she doesn't want to support you and doesn't want your book to succeed. If favor comes at you from one direction, jealousy will come from another direction to counter that favor. Normally, this doesn't bother me, but for whatever reason, I felt the sting of this rejection. Maybe it was because it was coming from a couple of women who I once thought highly of, but the problem wasn't necessarily them. While they had their issues, it was my responsibility, according to Proverbs 4:23, to guard my heart, and I'd failed to do that.

I spent quite a bit of time wrestling with that offense, but I remained prayerful and I asked the Lord to help and keep me. I didn't want to respond the wrong way, and I remained fully aware of the fact that I was experiencing rejection, offense and everything that comes with them. At the same time, I realized that I hadn't fully crucified my flesh because their actions should not have bothered me the way that they did. To my shame, I found myself treating them the way I felt they'd treated me (for a brief stint), and this was not right. Eventually, I repented and committed to showing them the love of Christ, even when I don't receive that love in return. A day or two later, I had the dream. The dream was all about competition, but again, I was at some award ceremony at a camp retreat, and there were a lot of people outside waiting to see if they'd won. And I was thrust into two categories that I hadn't signed up for, and I'd won! I wasn't competing in those categories, but somehow, I was drafted into the competition. What was God saying? It's simple. It was a dream about favor. God was showing me that while I hadn't started the fights, He'd already given me the victory because I'd been pulled into them. How so? When people feel the need to compare themselves to you, they then feel the need to compete with you. When they compete, they enter you into competitions that you haven't signed up for. All you did was show up and try to be the best version of yourself, not realizing that someone was lurking in the shadows nearby looking for a reason to justify his or her hatred of you. I'd gotten pulled into something that I hadn't signed up for, but in the end, I chose not to fight back. I chose to forgive. When you do this, God enters the fight on your behalf.

I'd entered the ring with the spirit of rejection, and I'd won, but not before I had been knocked down a few times! How so? I'd rejected rejection or, better yet, I'd castrated rejection.

In other words, I took away its ability to reproduce itself in my life. At first, I didn't reject it because I hadn't guarded my heart. I was well on my way to failing the test because I just couldn't understand why I was in a middle of a cold war with other believers. But I'd made a decision to stop feeling sorry for myself and just forgive! God also used this event to minister to me about standards. Oxford Language defines the word "standard" as "an idea or thing used as a measure, norm, or model in comparative evaluations." Whenever you place a person on any type of pedestal, that person becomes a standard. Don't get me wrong, when I say pedestal, I don't mean that you idolize the person or esteem to be like that person in totality; what I mean is that the person assumes a lead in your heart in a specific category. For example, you may decide that one of your co-workers is a gentle and intelligent woman. This is a standard; it's what you expect from her because this is what she's consistently demonstrated on the job. And you may say that you want to be as kind as she is. In other words, she serves as a representative or a standard of kindness to you. But what if God wanted you to have a higher standard or a greater degree of love than she has? The answer is simple—He may allow you to experience disappointment so that you can stop looking up to her in that area. He may allow you to experience rejection so that He can redirect your focus, and whenever you experience this, you have to pray, guard your heart and forgive with all of your might! This is because a standard represents a height, a width and a depth; these are all boundaries and limitations that determine how far you'll go in life and how far you'll go in God. So, whenever you aspire to reach, for example, the height of someone's character, you may be severely limiting what God wants and intends to do in your life. God may want you to go higher, to go further and to go deeper than the person you are looking up to. Understand that boundaries aren't just about keeping the wrong people out of your life or at a safe distance. God also uses boundaries as measuring sticks, and whenever you aspire to be a midget in an area where He has called you to be a giant, He will allow you to experience rejection in that area. Again, this is so that you'll redirect your eyes away from that particular person and find another individual to pattern yourself after.

Rejection comes to make you feel inadequate, unworthy and inferior to others. The enemy has weaponized rejection, both perceived and actual, in his attempt to gain access to the most intimate part of you, and that is your heart. This is why God told you to guard it. To guard something means to protect or shield it from an attack. In other words, we have to place a boundary around our minds, and one way to do this is by being mindful of and prayerful about the people we look up to. Never esteem a person you haven't studied and prayed about, regardless of whatever accomplishments that person has made! This is especially true if you are empathic or, better yet, prophetic. Prophetic people are incredibly sensitive, and whenever we experience a spike in our emotions, we often make decisions in those moments based on how we feel. Think about romantic relationships. If you're prophetic, it's pretty easy for someone to "love bomb" you; that is, if you haven't yet learned to be discerning and guard your heart. Wikipedia defines "love bombing" as "an attempt to influence a person by demonstrations of attention and affection. It can be used in different ways and for either positive or negative purposes." Love bombing is the attempt of an individual (more than likely a narcissist) to hijack the most intimate places of your heart in a short span of time. This allows the narcissist to quickly establish value in your life before he or she begins to devalue, manipulate and control you. It creates an imbalance in your perspective, whereas, the narcissist teaches you to see yourself as a peasant or someone unworthy of his or her attention and/or affection, all the while, seeing the narcissist as a royal presence in your life. This leads to you feeling like your life has little to no value unless the narcissist is both present in your life and pleased with your decisions. This creates what I call the seesaw effect. In this, you are always on the low end of the seesaw, lifting up the narcisstic personality, and as long as you keep that individual on a pedestal, you are awarded with attention, affection, and ultimatey, affirmation. Whenever you deny your own needs and desires, and you praise the narcissist, the individual will occasionally reward you by lowering himself or herself, all the while, lifting you up or, in most cases, balancing the seesaw. This typically looks like the narcissist spending a considerable amount of time with or money on you, or the narcissist openly acknowledging you as someone who is significant in his or her life. It could be a simple tag on Facebook, for example, someone may post a status that reads, "Make me laugh! Tell me something crazy that happened to you this year!" And the narcissist may comment under the post with, "That time (insert your name here) got chased by a poodle while trying to race me." In this, the narcissist has publicly acknowledged spending time with you and experiencing an event with you that the narcissist considers to be, at minimum, memorable. This is significant to you because of how you see the person, after all, he or she never publicly addresses you. But this is a reward, and it is designed to make the relationship appear to be working in your favor or, at minimum, balanced. It is designed to wet your pallette or make you crave more of the narcissist's affirmation. In other words, all those days and nights of holding up the narcissist's needs and desires above your own are occasionally rewarded, and the reward (to you) may appear to be significant. Again, the ultimate reward is affirmation. After this, you are expected to lift the narcissist back up, but this time, even higher than before, but whenever you begin to grow weary or question the narcissist's motives, the narcissist will suddenly get off the seesaw and leave you alone for a few days, weeks or months. In other words, you are placed on punishment; that is, until you realize the error of your ways. You may potentially go years investing in this relationship, always convincing yourself that the reward will be greater than the pain you're experiencing. It won't. Instead, the spirit of rejection will use all the time that you invest in that relationship, all the while neglecting yourself, to burrow itself deeper and deeper into your subconscious, where it will continue to devalue and degrade you; that is, until you find yourself looking up to or esteeming the lowest of people, and by "low," I mean people with little to no moral compass.

Your soul is comprised of your mind, will and emotions. The door to your soul, of course, would be your mind. The mind has levels to it, which are the conscious, subconscious and unconscious. The gate is the conscious mind; I call it the waiting room of the heart. Everything that enters the waiting room sits in the realm of thought and imagination; these are beliefs that you haven't yet labeled as truths or lies. They are still under consideration or still under review. Most thoughts age-out in the waiting room, meaning, they sit on the conscious level for so long that they become familiar to you. This causes you to trust those thoughts without testing them. Consequently, most of them will retire into the subconscious where they'll serve as "optional beliefs." Optional beliefs are theories that you are assuming to be true, even though you can't prove them. For example, you may find yourself saying, "Some people believe that Borderline Personality Disorder and Bipolar Disorder are one and the same, but because of capitalism, pyschologists and psychiatrists simply took two degrees of the same disease and labeled them differently. Simply put, Bipolar Disorder is BPD, but on a milder spectrum." This sounds intelligible, but you're no scientist, psychologist or psychiatrist! In other words, you haven't tested this theory, even though you've assumed it to be true. This is an optional belief, meaning that it is a well accepted theory of yours.

In the waitng room of your subconscious, you will find all types of lies, truths and fantasies, all waiting their turns to be tested. Most of them will never be confronted or tested. Most will age-out of the conscious and enter the subconscious as optional beliefs; these are theories or, better yet, assumptions, but some of them will die in the waiting room. These are the thoughts that you aren't really considering, either because you're not interested, or you don't necessarily believe them. Nevertheless, if you don't test them, they'll remain dormant in the thought-realm; this is because they have not been cast down. And every time a thought, an imagination or a theory comes to the forefront of your mind, you are given the option to test it. This means that it's up for consideration. If you accept it as truth, it then enters your subconscious as a truth; if you reject it as a lie, you cast it down from the conscious level, but you'll file a report of sorts in your subconscious, labeling the information as false. What this does is prevents the information from reentering your conscious to be tested again; that is, unless it comes with new information. This is how our immune systems are setup. Anytime anything foreign enters your body, your white blood cells will rush to that area to confront the foreign invader. They will surround the bacteria, virus or whatever it is, and begin to kill it. This is similar to what takes place in the waiting rooms of our souls. One of the reasons that we should be avid students of the Word of God is so that we can ingest the truth, and the truth can make us free. What this means is, whenever we are filled with truth, that truth will immediately surround and kill any lie that enters the subconscious. But if we have no information in a specific area, a void is formed. This void represents a dark spot or an empty room. This is where unclean spirits love to hide themselves. If you have no information in a specific area, it will be easy for you to accept a lie as a truth, and just like viruses, whenever a lie enters the subconscious, it then begins to reproduce itself. This means that your conscious mind is the battleground of your soul. Once a lie enters the subconscious, it then begins to behave like white blood cells; in other words, it'll serve to test any new information that enters your conscious mind. It will then cast out and reject the truth, but it'll defend most of the false information that you're presented with. This is why deceived people will believe just about any and everything that makes no sense to people who are mentally and emotionally healthy. The more lies a person believes, the less sane that person will be. This is why people who are schizophrenic, for example, say and believe some of the silliest things, and this is also why it is hard to convince such a person that what he or she is believing isn't true. I've counseled people who believed that their co-workers were after them, their family was out to get them, and their neighbors were plotting against them. I've counseled people who believed that the entire United States government was after them. I remember being hired by a woman who genuinely believed that the entire Nation of Islam was hacking into her computer just to monitor her activities. What happened to these people? Some of them were born into families where mental illness was prevalent, but many of them became mentally and spiritually unstable in their young adult lives; this is because they neglected to guard their hearts. In other words, they didn't test the information in the waiting room of their minds before they accepted that information as true. Consequently, the lies they embraced began to eat away at everything in their subconscious that made them stable. This caused them to become suspicious, distrusting and fearful of others. Of course, this is more than a mental illness, it is oftentimes spiritual as well. This is because the unconscious mind is the automatic response system of the soul; it houses trauma, memories, habits and repressed feelings. This is the part of you that you cannot consciously access. And of course, what Satan wants to do is toss a bunch of darts at your conscious, hoping that you'll adopt them as truths; this way, they can enter your subconscious where they'll begin to burrow themselves deeper and deeper until they've caused damage to your automatic response mechanism (your unconscious mind). Do you see why God told you to guard your heart or, better yet, place boundaries around your belief system? How do you do this?

Think about every scripture as an individual soldier waiting to join your army, but in order for this to happen, you have to:
1. Study the scripture.
2. Believe the Word.
3. Activate the Word.

How do you activate the Word? By speaking and applying it. The more soldiers (scriptures) you have in your army, the more effective you'll be whenever the enemy engages you in warfare. At the same time, it is important to note that you can have soldiers that you're not using, for example, you may know what the Word says about unforgiveness, but the minute someone offends you, you may find yourself struggling to forgive that person. So, while Ephesians 4:32 is sitting in your subconscious waiting to be deployed, you may have elected to engage another soldier, Vengeance. "Vengeance is mine, saith the Lord!" Nevertheless, in your fury, you may find yourself utilizing vengeance to teach your offender a lesson. What this means is that Ephesians 4:32 has been benched, while you've decided to fight wood with fire. This provokes God to defend the other person because once Vengeance enters the fight, it is no longer balanced. Isaiah 59:19 reads, "So shall they fear the name of the LORD from the west, and his glory from the rising of the sun. When the enemy shall come in like a flood, the Spirit of the LORD shall lift up a standard against him." Please note that whenever you become vengeful, you are partnering with Satan to hurt, harm or humiliate another person. This means that you pervert the use of vengeance. Additionally, the standard that God raises up is a boundary. The boundary isn't just there to protect the other person, it's also there to protect you. How so? Galatians 6:7 reads, "Be not deceived; God is not mocked: for whatsoever a man soweth, that shall he also reap." Whatever you sow into the life of that person, you plant and legalize in your own life. This is to say that memorizing the Word is half the battle!

Guard your heart. In short, place boundaries around your ears and eyes. And understand this—sometimes, the greatest and most effective weapon that the enemy has is rejection. As I mentioned earlier, I found myself being tested and attacked by this spirit recently, and I almost failed the test! Nevertheless, despite what I felt and despite what I experienced, I made a choice to not allow that thing to go any further than it had already gone. I renounced rejection, asked the Lord to help me to forgive the people, and finally, I activated that love by extending kindness to them. After this, God gave me a visual of what I had just done; He gave me a dream! And in that dream, I had been drafted into two competitions that I hadn't signed up for, and even though I'd tried to be humble and back out of those competitions, I'd won. The message He was sending to me was clear—whenever the enemy uses people to hurt or offend you, respond with love. This is what provokes God to respond to them. This is how you guard your heart, and this is how you render Satan powerless.

UNDER SIEGE

"He that hath no rule over his own spirit is like a city that is broken down, and without walls" (Proverbs 25:28). This scripture can be used in many contexts, for example, other translations say that a man who cannot control his temper is like a city without walls, but anger is one of the many human experiences that we all share. Therefore, the true nature of this scripture is not only about controlling yourself in moments of outrage, but dealing with legalities. Notice here that the author used the word "rule" and then he referenced one of the dimensions of a man: his spirit. The spirit rules the soul and the body or, at least, this is the way it's supposed to be. Keep in consideration that there are three dimensions to the soul; they are the mind, will and emotions. The mind (or heart) is comprised of three levels; they are:

Conscious Mind
Subconscious Mind
Unconscious Mind

The conscious mind deals with anything that is engaging your attention at any given moment, whether you can see, hear, taste, touch or smell it. The subconscious is where you store memories; this is your action/reaction center, and your unconscious mind is the part of you that you cannot control;

this area of your heart deals with trauma and controls your breathing. What is breath? Pneuma or spirit.

When the enemy wants to advance against a person, he has to first engage that person's conscious mind. It can be as subtle as a song on the radio or some random stranger insisting to pay for your lunch. Satan's goal is to build a siege around the unconscious mind; he can't overtake this part, but he can, at minimum, build a siege around it. The goal is to get you to dry up spiritually, whereas, you're no longer hearing from God, you're constantly being bound by demonic forces and your mind is constantly at war with itself.

- **Proverbs 17:22:** A merry heart doeth good like a medicine: but a broken spirit drieth the bones.
- **Proverbs 18:14:** The spirit of a man will sustain his infirmity; but a wounded spirit who can bear?
- **Exodus 6:9:** And Moses spake so unto the children of Israel: but they hearkened not unto Moses for anguish of spirit, and for cruel bondage.

If Satan can get past the waiting room of your soul (the conscious mind) and enter the subconscious arena, he has successfully bound you. But the subconscious arena has levels as well. The password to each level is called intimacy, high level offense or trauma. Intimacy is the easiest way to navigate and ascend through the ranks of a man's soul, but it isn't the shortest route. Trauma is. As a matter of fact, if an event is traumatic enough, it'll be stored in the third level or, better yet, the unconscious mind. This is the area that Satan wants to attack the most because it controls your survival. So, a city without walls is pretty much a land or region without any measure of protection; it is a spirit that has no boundaries. It's a spirit that's open for the enemy to attack. Again, the enemy cannot enter the spirit of a believer, so his goal is to oppress it or build a siege wall around it. But to do this, he must ascend every rank of the soul. One of the most common routes, of course, is called romantic warfare. This is when a man or a woman convinces his or her insignificant other to lower his or her walls, also known as guards or boundaries. This is often done through love bombing (overwhelming the person with positive emotions in a short amount of time by giving that person excessive amounts of attention and affection), using tear gas (threatening the leave the person or by suddenly not answering the person's calls) or through espionage (marrying or promising to marry the person in an attempt to learn more about the person; this is solely done for one's own benefit, and not the benefit of the marital unit). This is why God warns us to guard our hearts, but Satan has convinced and even trained us to be hearers of the Word, not doers. Through our educational system, we've been taught reading comprehension, whereas, we are triggered to read words, but not necessarily conceive or apply them. This is why we often have to read a book or an article three times before we learn to truly apply it to our lives. This is also why God also told us to "write the vision and make it plain." According to Dr. Gail Matthews of Dominican University (California), you are 42 percent more likely to achieve your goals if you write them down. This was

39

taken from the research that she'd done with 270 students. No military plans an attack in their heads; they write it down, draw maps and discuss their methods of attack with their troops.

Satan plans to get as close to your unconscious mind as he possibly can. But in order for this to happen, he has to get you to enter some an agreement with him. He does this through deception. Whatever you don't know <u>can</u> kill you. God says it this way, "My people are destroyed for lack of knowledge" (Hosea 4:6). But Satan rarely tells a person to remove their walls; he advances by getting them to move their walls. Let me explain.

Imagine this. It's 1247 A.D. during the medieval era. You're a knight employed by the king to run a sector of his military. You head off into a room with other military officials. The king wants to build a new wall around the kingdom, and you guys are coming together to look at the new blueprint so that you can compare it with the current blueprint. One of the dukes opens the scroll and rolls it out onto a large table. Immediately, you notice that the walls seem to be closing in—literally. A voice shatters the silence. "It seems like we're losing ground," says one of the other knights. "The walls seem to be getting closer to the castle. Why is that?" The Admiral speaks up. "The king has been receiving some offers and complaints regarding the wall. One of the neighboring kings complained that we simply have too much territory around us. He complained that our walls were too high, our land was too plentiful, and our military was too strong. So, in order for his kingdom to continue allying with ours, he has requested that we pull the walls in closer, just as a showmanship of trust. Another king said that the hill our castle is on is already high enough, so we don't need so much military presence. He complained that one of his Dukes came over to speak with us one day, and he had to go through so many levels of security just to get to the king. So, the king spoke with his advisors, and as an act of good faith, he's decided to lessen our security's presence and pull the walls in closer to the castle. He also wants the new walls to be two feet shorter than the original ones." You look at the guys in utter dismay and grunt in frustration. This isn't the first time the king has listened to the complaints of his so-called allies; this isn't the first time he's moved the walls closer to the castle.

One day, someone sounds the alarms of war. As it turns out, the two kings who'd been complaining now have their military surrounding your castle. You rush to the wall, only to see the opposing military less than a mile away. They're strong and plentiful, and it's clear that your kingdom doesn't have the strength or the manpower to overcome the two kingdoms that have allied themselves together to destroy your kingdom, plus, your new walls aren't high enough to protect the castle. Nevertheless, you give them all of the fight that you have in you until your kingdom is no more.

What happened here? It's simple. The king was foolish and

so were his advisors. Understand that this is EXACTLY how the enemy advances against God's people! Warfare doesn't always look and sound like warfare. When those two kings shook hands with your king in an alliance, little did he know, he was in the throngs of warfare. He passively entered into an agreement that was designed to take him down! The same is true whenever the wrong man approaches a woman who's set her heart to serving and pleasing the Lord. The minute he lays his eyes on her, she is in the midst of a battle, but she doesn't yet know this. The battle has only intensified and gotten closer whenever he approaches her and says, "Hello beautiful lady. I've been watching you for a while now and I'd love to get to know you. Can I call you sometime?" If she gives him her number, he advances a few steps, not for her but against her. When he takes her on a date, he's made a few more advancements in her heart and, at the same time, against her heart. "Guard your heart, for out of it pours the issues of life!" God's voice echoes over the course of eternity, but she's caught up in the man's beautiful eyes, his nearly perfect smile and the fact that he goes to church. With every phone conversation, he advances in her heart and against her heart. Next, they share their first kiss and he graduates from the waiting room of her heart (the conscious mind) and makes his way into the depths of her subconscious. Now, she can't stop thinking of him. If she could see in the realm of the spirit, she would see demons using soul ties like zip ties to bind her. She'd see the enemy tying her to a man who's tied to 78 other women that he's broken and bound. She'd see her new lover in his dark bedroom nearly every night, with only the light emitting from his television set, and if she were to look up, she'd see the images that he's filling his soul with. She'd see his addiction to porn. And if her eyes were to open a little more, she'd find the women (and a few guys) who've been spiritually tied up by this guy and tossed into the closets of his soul, only to have their skeletons pulled out whenever his lustful appetite for them begins to flare up. But she's blind. So, all she sees is the man in the dress shoes passing out communion cups at her church. All she hears are the "Hallelujahs" and the "Amens" that he belches out whenever their pastor says something revelatory. All she feels are the deceptive sounds of her bound heart, sounding like sweet melodies on a rainy day. She calls it "in love," but God calls it bondage.

One day, the man calls her up on the phone and passively begins to threaten leaving the relationship. He's been cold and distant lately, and her heart can't seem to bear the thought of losing him. "What's going on?" she asks, hoping that he'll say that he's just been tired or he'll tell her about some bad event that he's been enduring; this way, she'll know that his sudden change of heart isn't necessarily a change of plans. "My aunt died," he says. She lets out a silent sigh of relief. Of course, she's not happy with the news; she's simply relieved because he seems to be giving a reasonable explanation as to why he's been absent from her life. "I'm sorry to hear that. Are you okay? When did she die? Why didn't you call me? Do you need anything?" Her voice is annoying to him at this point, nevertheless, he answers.

"I'm ...Yeah, I'm okay, but I messed up. You there? I said I messed up. Saturday night, I felt like I needed somebody to just come over to my house and wrap their arms around me. I felt like I was about to lose my mind, but I knew I couldn't call you. I knew that you'd be all in the pastor's ear, talking about, 'Joe tried to get me to come over to his house,' or 'Joe ain't really saved,' so I didn't bother. I ended up calling an ex of mine and she agreed to come over and comfort me. But I felt bad about it, so I called her back and told her not to come." In other words, he's manipulating her in an attempt to get her to lift her boundaries all the more. Her boundaries are keeping him from making the advances he really wants to make. "Joe, I'm not like that!" she counters. "You could have just called me, and I would have been there! You didn't even give me a fair chance! You just immediately assumed that I wouldn't care about what you're going through, and you are wrong! I do care!" Joe smiles mischievously, but she can't see him because they're speaking over the phone. "Yes ma'am. I'm sorry. What are you doing right now? Can you stop by? I could really use a shoulder to cry on." Nine months later, she's experiencing the greatest pain of her life. "Push!" screams one of the doctors. "I can see the head crowning!" She lets out another scream as she pushes her son into this world. As a single mother, she has long left her church because of the shame she felt every time she walked through the doors and had to look her ex in the face. The last straw had come when she'd witnessed him doing to another young woman what he'd done to her. "Hallelujah," he'd shouted, while standing next to the beautiful first-time visitor. "Come on, pastor! You're preaching!" At that moment, she realized that she hadn't been the first of his victims, nor would she be the last. "Why is he even allowed to serve?" she'd questioned her pastor before making her decision to leave her church. The pastor's answer shocked her. "We let you serve, didn't we? He didn't have sex with himself. You are equally responsible for what transpired between the two of you. Take accountability and learn from this. He's still a work in progress, and obviously, so are you. He manipulated you to get what he wanted, but my problem with you is the fact that you were able to be so easily manipulated. So, should we seat every man who successfully manipulates you if he refuses to commit afterward? Why are you trying to diminish your own role and responsibility in what you say happened to you? Let's be clear. You're not mad at him for being a fornicator; you're not even mad that he's serving, because you served alongside him and didn't say a word when you thought he was your husband-to-be, but the minute he broke your heart, you decided to use the same scriptures that you hadn't followed in an attempt to get us to make him sit down or potentially run him out of this church? No! The both of you were wrong! Period! Now, you both have to deal with the consequences, but let's get this straight—if I sit him down, I'm sitting you down as well. I hope I made myself clear."

What happened to the woman in question? The enemy kept advancing against her and getting her to take down the walls that she had up, walls that were designed to guard her heart (see Proverbs 4:23). And the more those boundaries came down or were pushed backwards, the more the enemy advanced, but again, warfare doesn't always look or sound like warfare. Consider the fate of the king in the aforementioned story. When his two "allies" complained about the height and distance of his kingdom's walls and the strength of his military, he was in the midst of warfare, but because they disguised themselves as allies, he was easily deceived. Everyone in his kingdom paid the ultimate price for his need to please. Every man, woman or spirit that demands or suggests that you have too many boundaries and that your walls are too high is complaining because you're making it difficult for them to manipulate and attack you. Ever since I started truly and wholeheartedly serving the Lord, forsaking the world and all it has to offer, I've experienced the silence that comes with having and enforcing boundaries. I've also heard people joke around, saying that I'll never marry because my walls are too high or (my favorite) because I try to stay within the confines of God's will. Of course, these "jokes" come from well-meaning people who don't personally know me; they just know that they've never heard me cursing, they've never seen me in a man's face flirting, they've never seen me angry and they always see me producing for the Kingdom of God, so they don't know what to make of me, and I'm honestly okay with that. I don't try to defend myself, nor do I lower my walls (expectations). I just giggle because I know that they are speaking from (for lack of a better phrase) the floor of the castle that they live on. If you live on the upper level of a castle, you will be able to see more from your window than the people who live a few floors beneath you. This isn't to degrade them because they are likely great people, but it is to say that our perspectives are different. They were talking about what it would take to get a man on their level, a man who would be scared away by the boundaries that I have surrounding my heart, for example:

1. No sex before marriage.
2. No kissing before the pastor says, "You may now kiss the bride."
3. He can't come to my house and I'm not coming to his.
4. We cannot and will not be alone together unless we're in a public place.
5. He has to be committed to God wholeheartedly. I'm not interested in double-minded men. This means that his level of consecration has to outmatch or supersede my own.

Now, to someone who lives on another floor of the castle, those few requirements are too much to ask of another human being. So, when they advise me, they're trying to advise me on how to get a man on their level. I don't want the guy, so I don't listen. I teach what I call the Pyramid Effect of relationships. Look at the pyramid below to get a better understanding.

As you can see, the most common area is where you'll find babes in Christ. This is where we all start off. You'll also notice on the chart that there are boundaries separating each area or level. These are the boundaries that we sense whenever we are talking with people. For example, when someone starts a conversation with me and they abruptly end the conversation, this doesn't mean that they are bad people; it could mean that we are on two different levels, therefore, we don't comprehend one another well. I speak against (most) secular music. I don't believe Christians should have trash playing in their ears. The Lord gave me a term for this music some time ago; He called it "slave music." But there are many believers who would (passionately and violently) disagree with this. I teach this concept: if the music tells you that it's okay to sin against God (directly or indirectly) or if it promotes sin, it shouldn't be playing in your ears. It's the doctrine of demons set to a beat! But what I had to learn was that the level of consecration God called me to isn't necessarily the level of consecration that He has called others to. Are there benefits to each level? Indeed! Anytime you're willing to sacrifice something you want for the glory and promotion of God's Kingdom, He upgrades or, better yet, promotes you. This doesn't mean that a prophet will become an apostle; it simply means that a prophet may find himself or herself in an uncommon area, hearing more from God and being used more by God than other prophets. "Then answered Peter and said unto him, Behold, we have forsaken all, and followed thee; what shall we have therefore? And Jesus said unto them, Verily I say unto you, That ye which have followed me, in the regeneration when the Son of man shall sit in the throne of his glory, ye also shall sit upon twelve thrones, judging the twelve tribes of

Israel. And every one that hath forsaken houses, or brethren, or sisters, or father, or mother, or wife, or children, or lands, for my name's sake, shall receive an hundredfold, and shall inherit everlasting life" (Matthew 17:27-29).

Every time you give something up that you want to keep, and you do this for God's glory, you provoke Him to respond. Now, giving something up that you are in love with isn't easy. This is why it's called a sacrifice. Sacrificial offerings, when given in love and cheerfulness, will often strengthen your relationship with God because it shows God that He can trust you. This means that you don't have to be "called" to a level of consecration to partake of it. If you want more of God, give Him more of you!

Notice on the chart that there is a standard or common area for believers. This is where you'll find most believers today, and it's not a bad place, so please don't think that if you're there that you're double-minded. No. Double mindedness and immaturity are not one and the same. We all go through levels during the maturation process, and for some of us, we stop growing the minute or moment we decide that we're okay with where we're at. There are many called people who got stuck on this level, but remember what Jesus said in Matthew 22. "For many are called, but few are chosen." Another word for called is invited. God has invited us all to mature; He has invited us all to forsake the lusts of our flesh, the trappings of this world and the overwhelming, almost invincible desire to fit in, as these are all prisons. But He chooses certain people; sometimes from the pool of the ones He's invited, other times, from their mother's wombs, to lead His people. God always uses who He chooses, and the more we avail ourselves to be used by Him, the more He raises us up. Another word for this is maturity. All the same, He begins to trust us with more wisdom and revelation. Wisdom is the equivalent of spiritual wealth. As He's doing this, He's (in a sense) causing us to move from one region of thought to another.

In every new region of thought, you will find a new set of boundaries, expectations and rewards. If you don't wrestle with God regarding the level of sanctification that He's calling you to, He'll continue to reveal Himself to you. One day, you may find yourself in one of the uncommon areas (see chart) wondering how you got there. Now, everyone you encounter is somewhere on the map of this chart. Believers who are still babes in Christ or are still in love with the world will often sound, think and behave like the world. If you're in an uncommon area, you run the risk of offending one of them if you don't choose your words carefully or know when and how to navigate or end a conversation with them. This is why God said in Matthew 18:6, "But whoso shall offend one of these little ones which believe in me, it were better for him that a millstone were hanged about his neck, and that he were drowned in the depth of the sea." He wasn't just referring to natural children, the Lord was dealing with the learned in regard to the unlearned. A baby Christian is just one decision away from returning to the world, but a believer who is maturing has to learn to not intentionally offend the new (or not-so-new) convert. Jesus warned His disciples in Luke 17:1 this way, "Then said he unto the disciples, It is impossible but that offences will come: but woe unto him, through whom they come!" Now, please understand that offending believers, whether mature or immature, is inevitable. You will offend people, but what our Lord is dealing with here are the people He's entrusted with His sheep, only to have them become self-righteous and prideful, causing them to chase away the souls He assigned them to cover.

If you'll review the chart again, you'll notice that there is a midway point, a place for mature believers; while it's in the middle of the pyramid, it is the bottom step or beginner's step for leadership. Leaders cannot be standard believers; instead, they have to go and grow beyond the norm. As the leader continues to ascend, he or she becomes more and more uncommon, which also means that most people won't be able to relate to or fully understand that leader. Everyone reasons according to the level that they're on, so when an uncommon leader makes a decision that a common believer doesn't understand, the believer can either choose to pray about it and study more or the believer can get offended, go into the common area and gather around people who have the same perspective as he or she does. This is why most leaders get stuck in the middle of the spectrum; many reason that they don't want to be so far gone that they can't reason with the sheep, others reason that venturing too far into the heart and will of God is a recipe for loneliness (another sacrifice leaders make involves relationships; the less people understand you, the more they'll avoid you). On the other hand, the more God can use you, the more people He'll reach through you. This is where the word "agreement" comes to play. It is the heart and desire of God to use you at your greatest capacity, but He will not use you beyond the measure that you agree to be used by Him. When and if you agree to let Him make you uncommon and to use you beyond your imaginations, you've just entered an agreement or contract of sorts with Him. Sure, the warfare on every level intensifies as you elevate, however, it doesn't always feel unbearable because you're wiser. In other words, your enemies get bigger, but because you've grown as well, they don't always appear to be bigger or, at least, not in your eyes. This means that you have the measure of faith needed to overcome every adversary that crosses into your life.

THE POWER AND BENEFITS OF BOUNDARIES

Lucifer stood in Heaven with a host of angels backing him. His belly was swollen with all the lies he'd told himself, some of which had already begun to crown. He wanted to give birth in the place that he called home so that he could establish his dominion there, but God wasn't about to allow it. With all of his supporters armed and deceived, Lucifer gave the command. "Fight!" Little did they know, there was no way that they could win the battle. Moments later, he would find himself falling, alongside the angels he'd convinced to back him. The fall seemed to go on forever! They tried to spread their wings, but their once beautiful wings were gone. Now, unable to defy gravity and lift themselves up, they found themselves helplessly tumbling into the Earth's realm. They'd trespassed against the Lord God, and because of this, they'd lost their places in Heaven. They'd gone from being beautiful beings of light, filled with love and worship to becoming dark, hideous beings. Unplugged from their former Source, they became void of light; in other words, they found themselves naked; they'd lost their heavenly bodies, and now, they were hideous balls of gas.

Meanwhile, Eve found herself staring at a foreign tree in the Garden of Eden. It was beautiful to look at, and its fruits were big, ripe and covered with dew. They looked delectable! Eve looked at the serpent that had been enticing her, and then, she looked back at the tree. Now on the edge of her sanity, she just needed just one last push and she'd find herself pregnant with a lie. "You will be like God, knowing all things," Satan said as he smiled mischievously. That was it. Eve reached into the tree and snapped one of the lowest hanging fruits from one of its branches. She then opened her mouth and shoved the lie into it. She began to move the lie around in her mouth as she chewed it. Oh, how sweet it was! Moments later, her belly began to swell. Excited, but confused, she immediately went to find her husband. "Here, taste this," she said. Adam didn't ask any questions. He knew where the fruit had come from, but Eve had bitten into it and she seemed to be fine. As a matter of fact, she'd never looked so confident in her life. Adam bit into the forbidden fruit, and immediately, his belly began to swell. The couple were now pregnant, but God was not the father of what they were carrying.

"Get out!" God's voice echoed and shook every tree in the Garden. God was not about to allow the couple to give birth to the lies they'd swallowed on His private property. And just like Lucifer, the couple found themselves experiencing what felt like a never-ending fall. *Thump!* It was almost like waking up from a very bad falling dream, only when they woke up, they were no longer surrounded by the plushness of the clouds or the enchanting smells of fruits, flowers and dew. Instead, they woke up in a foreign land. The couple would eventually give birth to Cain, followed by the birth of their son, Abel. Of course, Cain would kill Abel and life as we know it began to take form.

"How did this happen? I don't understand!" The desperation in Eve's voice was evident. Jesus would possibly answer this question thousands of years later in the book of Matthew. He introduced us to the parable of the weeds; it reads, "Another parable put he forth unto them, saying, The kingdom of heaven is likened unto a man which sowed good seed in his field: But while men slept, his enemy came and sowed tares among the wheat, and went his way. But when the blade was sprung up, and brought forth fruit, then appeared the tares also. So the servants of the householder came and said unto him, Sir, didst not thou sow good seed in thy field? From whence then hath it tares? He said unto them, An enemy hath done this. The servants said unto him, Wilt thou then that we go and gather them up? But he said, Nay; lest while ye gather up the tares, ye root up also the wheat with them. Let both grow together until the harvest: and in the time of harvest I will say to the reapers, Gather ye together first the tares, and bind them in bundles to burn them: but gather the wheat into my barn."

Of course, the above story is a fictitious or overly exaggerated account of what happened before and after the great fall of man. And we know that the aforementioned parable can be translated in many ways, but let's look at it from an unexplored angle. Is it possible that the Tree of the

Knowledge of Good and Evil hadn't been planted in the Garden by God, but it simply represented the presence of evil in the midst of good? What if Satan planted it, after all, he clearly had access to the Garden? Or what if everything that took place in the spirit had to express itself in the natural? Whatever the answer may be, what we do know is that God placed a boundary around the tree, telling the couple that it was off limits. You see, the Tree of the Knowledge of Good and Evil was powerless by itself. It was contained; it could not and would not reproduce itself without cross-pollination, however, when Eve ate from the tree, she became a conduit for Satan to reproduce his lies. She availed herself to become a womb or a vessel for lies to pass through. Of course, the same is true for Adam. Consequently, God evicted the couple from the Garden, before drawing a boundary around the Garden, prohibiting the couple from reentering it. This is similar to what He did with our unconscious minds once we got saved. Once we received the Holy Spirit, Satan could no longer possess us; he could only oppress us. Think of it this way—in the waiting room of your soul, there stands a lie or two. Also, in that waiting room are many facts and truths that you have tested and approved to go into your subconscious mind. This means that you have knowledge, but no understanding of somethings. Understanding comes when a truth in your subconscious validates some of the information in your conscious. When the two pair up, they produce a measure of understanding. Once you approve the information and send it from the waiting room of your soul, it will then go through your mental digestive system. From there, you'll extract the nutrients from the information. These nutrients are called revelation and wisdom. However, if you eat from the lies that are in your conscious waiting to be tested, that lie will be sweet at first, but bitter to your belly. Meaning, your soul will attempt to regurgitate it. This is the alarm of the soul going off, warning you that something has bypassed the conscious and is now on its way to the sacred place that is your heart. This alarm often sounds like worry, fear, anxiety, forgetfulness or the infamous butterflies in the stomach. If you don't vomit the lie out (reject it), it will then enter your subconscious, where it'll root itself and begin to attack many of the truths that have been established in your mind. For example, when Satan tempted Eve, he asked her, "Did God actually say, 'You shall not eat of any tree in the garden'?" She knew the truth, but this question was designed to dislodge the truth so that the lie could root itself. In that moment, she stopped believing God and she started believing Satan. "Therefore God gave them up in the lusts of their hearts to impurity, to the dishonoring of their bodies among themselves, because they exchanged the truth about God for a lie and worshiped and served the creature rather than the Creator, who is blessed forever! Amen" (Romans 1:24-25).

"Open your mouth," said Dr. Griffin. "Now, lift your tongue. Move it around for me. Okay, good. You can close your mouth now." Dr. Griffin turned off his flashlight and made his way out of the room. "Nurse, watch him for about five or ten minutes. He's a sneaky one," said the doctor to one of the male nurses standing behind him. Dr. Griffin was a psychiatrist at a local psychiatric hospital, and he'd just visited one of his patients by the name of Joe. Crazy Joe, as he would come to be known by some of the patients, had been diagnosed with Schizophrenia, Bipolar Disorder and Multiple Personality Disorder, along with a host of other issues. He was known for taking off all his clothes and proudly waltzing around his room as if he was dancing in a ballroom with the prettiest lady at the party. He'd stop after around thirty minutes and suddenly start crying, apologizing nonstop to his invisible dance partner and begging for another chance. "I didn't mean to step on your foot, my lady!" he'd scream in a fake British accent. "You're just so beautiful, I got caught up in your eyes! Please don't walk away! I need you! You complete me!" After this episode, he would normally collapse on the floor, curl up in the fetal position and stare at the door for around five minutes before crying hysterically. This is when doctors would go into the room and sedate him. Crazy Joe would have an episode like this once every three to four days. On other days, he'd just sit and stare at the wall or he'd sit on the toilet for hours and chirp like a bird. The world refers to Joe as a "maniac," but in the church, we know that he is a "demoniac." Of course, we all probably have an idea as to why Joe behaves the way that he does. Some people would guess that one or both of his parents were mentally unstable or maybe, something traumatic took place in his childhood or adulthood that drove him insane. And while both of these guesses are feasible, they don't necessarily deal with the root of Joe's mental illness; they possibly deal with the events that took place in the natural realm, but they don't explain what's happened to Joe spiritually. In Proverbs 18:14, the author asked the question, "The spirit of a man will sustain his infirmity; but a wounded spirit who can bear?" Let me suggest to you that a broken spirit is not always depression; depression is oftentimes one of the following:

1. The presence of purpose overwhelmed by the absence of action (procrastination).
2. A spirit man that's been starved of prayer and worship.
3. Mental warfare.
4. A soul longing for something or someone it cannot reach.
5. The splitting of a soul because of double-mindedness. When a person's soul has an invitation to the next season, but a comfort zone in the last season; this is when the soul is torn between two seasons.
6. Manipulation. When people try to coerce God (through tears) to give them whatever it is that they want, or they try to manipulate Him into letting them keep whatever it is that He is taking or has taken away from them.

The spirit is the third level of a human; when it has been wounded, its security system has been breached. Note that the enemy has to first engage the conscious mind, but his overall goal (as it relates to believers) is to build a siege wall around the spirit man. This wall is called pride. For example, the cities of old would often trade with other nations; this was how they sustained themselves. This was also how they built and strengthened alliances between themselves and other nations. When an enemy decided to take a city, one of the warfare tactics they discussed was possibly building a siege wall around that city if they had enough manpower to do so. Our spirit man is an information center; our spirit man communicates with God and hears back from God. When this doesn't happen, he begins to dry up. If this were to happen to you, you'd start craving something spiritual after a while. If you're not hearing from God, you'd start venturing off into other doctrines, looking for a way to appease your thirst. What you're unknowingly doing is feeling up the void or empty spaces (questions) in your belief system; in short, you're simply ushering the enemy closer and closer to your spirit man. As his team begins to get in position, they'd launch a series of attacks against your spirit. Since they can't enter in, they have to release what the Bible calls "fiery darts." Why fiery darts? The answer is in the scriptures. God said that Satan comes to kill, steal and destroy. What does fire do? It kills anything that's living, it robs a person of everything that they have and it destroys the evidence! Anything burned by fire cannot be restored! We thank God for the precious blood of Jesus which allows us to be restored, but the point is, when we see people who have lost the soundness of their minds, we are seeing people who have siege walls built around their spirits! This means that at some point in their lives, the enemy crept into their imaginations and made his way past their waiting rooms. He then sat in the second level (subconscious mind) and he continued his assault against the person's mind. The person had no defense in place to guard himself or herself from the attack. "He that hath no rule over his own spirit is like a city that is broken down, and without walls" (Proverbs 25:28).

Once the enemy was able to successfully build a siege wall around the soul of the person, he was able to launch a bunch of attacks, causing the person to either hallucinate or see mocking spirits disguising themselves as humans, animals, aliens or freaks of nature. So, can Crazy Joe be set free? Of course, he can! Consider the story of the man who had a legion of spirits. Mark 5:1-13; it reads, "And they came over unto the other side of the sea, into the country of the Gadarenes. And when he was come out of the ship, immediately there met him out of the tombs a man with an unclean spirit, who had his dwelling among the tombs; and no man could bind him, no, not with chains: Because that he had been often bound with fetters and chains, and the chains had been plucked asunder by him, and the fetters broken in pieces: neither could any man tame him. And always, night and day, he was in the mountains, and in the tombs, crying, and cutting himself with stones. But when he saw Jesus afar off, he ran and worshipped him, and cried with a loud voice, and said, What have I to do with thee, Jesus, thou Son of the most high God? I adjure thee by God, that thou torment me not. For he said unto him, Come out of the man, thou unclean spirit. And he asked him, What is thy name? And he answered, saying, My name is Legion: for we are many. And he besought him much that he would not send them away out of the country. Now there was there nigh unto the mountains a great herd of swine feeding. And all the devils besought him, saying, Send us into the swine, that we may enter into them. And forthwith Jesus gave them leave. And the unclean spirits went out, and entered into the swine: and the herd ran violently down a steep place into the sea, (they were about two thousand;) and were choked in the sea."

The doctors listed a lot of diseases and disorders that they said Joe has, but in truth, Joe is in demonic bondage; he is more than a maniac, he is a demoniac. I've seen a lot believers flirting with insanity over the last ten years. I've worked with a lot of ministries, so it goes without saying that I've met the sane, the insane and those who have a passport to insanity. Some of the cases that stand out to me the most are of a few women and men who'd either gone into witchcraft after having been in ministry for quite some time or turned completely against the Lord. One of the issues that they all had in common was that they weren't fully satisfied with God (remember, when the enemy is building a siege wall around the third level of a man's mind, he causes the man to dry up; this is what creates the thirst). One woman kept moving around, going from church to church in search for something; she would always end up offended and on the run again. Another woman wouldn't stop fornicating. She was so determined to be in a relationship that she'd serve

God while she was between relationships, but the minute she met a man, she would go right back into sexual immorality. The enemy had built a siege wall around her finances, so she'd become even more desperate to the point where she not only wanted a man for sex, but she was in desperate need of a second income. This put her in survivor's mode. One guy kept looking at other doctrines, trying to discover the totality of God (this is something the human mind cannot comprehend), and I'm not sure what happened to another woman, but she was convinced that the CIA, the FBI and the entire federal government was after her. (Honestly, I've met a few people like this). I remember meeting another woman who was sure that her neighbors and her coworkers were out to kill her. She kept quitting her jobs and moving because she was convinced that everyone around her was involved in some plot to take her life. Were these people devils disguising themselves as ministers? Not necessarily. Many of them were people who'd taken the Word of God for granted; they hadn't put on the whole armor of God, and they hadn't guarded their hearts. So, the enemy kept advancing against them until they became offended with the idea of serving YAHWEH or, at minimum, serving Him the way He wants to be served. Two of the women became witches, two continued to think that people were after them and the guy turned to a false religion. Of course, it goes without saying that some of these people clearly suffered from what medical doctors refer to as schizophrenia, and it is possible that they wrestled with this spirit before they'd even considered Christianity. Maybe it was a generational issue in their family. Then again, it may have been an event that occurred as a result of trauma. I think it's important to note that a lot of our trauma is the byproduct of our dissatisfaction with God. We put ourselves in harm's way while looking for love, looking for a good time or looking for one of the many void-fillers that we once medicated ourselves with. This may sound insensitive, after all, in the western world, we have labeled some truths as taboo, nevertheless, it is the truth that not only sets us free, but keeps us from going back into bondage. The point is a lot of what the world refers to as "crazy people" are prophetic souls who lost the soundness of their minds because of the choices they've made. If we promote this truth, more people would stay within the bounds of God's Word, and not allow the enemy to entice them to eat any of the forbidden fruits of this world.

Anytime you feel that God isn't enough, please note that it's time for you to go through a few rounds of deliverance. This means that the enemy has successfully breached your security. And this is okay. We all have to undergo maintenance; we all need regular bouts of deliverance. You should never entertain thoughts like:

- I need more friends because the ones I have are nobodies!
- I need to be married and quick! What's taking God so long?
- My pastors don't like me. It's time for me to find another church.

- I need to get close to that woman or that man because they'll help me to grow my name or my ministry.

These thoughts are often indicators that your mind is under attack; these thoughts indicate that you're not fully satisfied with God, and now, you're being tempted to go outside of God's will. You're beginning to plot on ways of elevating and/or delivering yourself. This is what Eve did. Satan said that by disobeying God, she'd become like God. In that moment, she wanted to elevate herself; she wanted power and influence. And don't get me wrong, there's nothing wrong with wanting to do better or surround yourself with better people, but you should always keep inventory of what's in your heart to ensure that your motives are pure. If you've recently gone through a breakup and you suddenly start fantasizing about being popular, chances are, you are being seduced by the enemy. It is always important that you match your imaginations with the events that triggered them; this way, you will know how to respond to your imaginations and you won't establish a set of plans or beliefs in your subconscious mind that open you up for demonic infestation.

HORIZONTAL BOUNDARIES VS. VERTICAL BOUNDARIES

Region:

- an area or division, especially part of a country or the world having definable characteristics but not always fixed boundaries (Google Online Dictionary).
- an indefinite area of the world or universe (Merriam Webster).
- a large indefinite area or range of something specified; sphere (Dictionary.com).
- an area of a country, especially one that has a particular characteristic or is known for something (Cambridge Dictionary).
- any large, indefinite, and continuous part of a surface or space (Collins Dictionary).
- A region is an area. A region can be geographic — like a part of a country. A region can be intellectual — like a region of the mind. There are also bodily regions — like abdominal, thoracic, and posterior (Vocabulary.com).

A region, in short, is a space that's been defined individually or corporately, but not legally. For example, a drug dealer can stand on the balcony of his apartment and shout, "This is my hood!" Now, in fact, the neighborhood does not belong to him; it's simply the area that he sells drugs in and has (verbally or violently) placed off limits to other drug dealers. Another drug dealer can be living downstairs from him, completely aware of his presence and his beliefs, but the guy may be under a completely different jurisdiction of thoughts—same demon, just a different perspective. So, he may be selling drugs without the knowledge of his neighbor. He's not moved by fear; instead, he chooses to sell drugs in that neighborhood as well, just outside of his neighbor's knowledge. Wouldn't this mean that he was afraid of his neighbor? To a prideful man, yes, but to a sensible person, the answer is an obvious no. He's not afraid of his neighbor, he's a criminal so he does what criminals do. While both men live in the same complex, selling drugs in the same communities, both men have different approaches to how they define what they believe to be theirs. Nevertheless, their beliefs are not facts; they are simply individually defined by each person. A woman may live on a completely different side of town who doesn't know the drug dealers. Her friend calls and announces that she's moving to her city. The woman then begins to warn her friend about certain regions or neighborhoods in that city that she says she should not move into. The neighborhood that the drug dealer claimed is one of them. He's defining the area using a different mode of measurement than she is. He's trying to claim territory for himself, but the woman is warning her friend about a bunch of rough areas that she should avoid at all costs. Now, the government doesn't acknowledge the neighborhood as being the drug dealer's neighborhood, even though the feds may acknowledge that it's an area that he's been lording himself over, so they may map it off and refer to it as a region so that they can easily identify it when communicating with one another.

The drug dealer may have started off selling drugs on the street he lives on. He advanced by claiming the neighboring streets as his own. Before long, he'd taken an entire neighborhood, but if you listen to him speak, you'll understand that he's planning to venture out even further. "We're gonna take the city!" he says to a few of the men who are selling drugs for him. Like the Admiral in the medieval times, he pulls out a map and points at the different streets and neighborhoods, detailing the name of the drug dealers in those areas. He lists the strengths and weaknesses of each drug dealer and the men strategize on how to take those neighborhoods for themselves. If they are successful, the drug dealer may start to advance against the city until he has scared off or corrupted most of the city's government officials. This is called warfare; again, it's when two or more people come together to strategize against another person, family or unit. This is when people plan to illegally cross boundaries in an attempt to conquer the minds and possessions of the people on the other side of that boundary. Now, if the law enforcement department remains incorruptible, they may be able to take down these drug dealers. But they can't do this without the community's cooperation. Let's review Amos 3:3 again. It states, "Can two walk together, except they be agreed?" If the people in those communities refuse to cooperate; if they are under another agreement called the "No Snitch Clause," their neighborhoods will continue to be riddled by crime; their daughters will continue to be raped and/or objectified while their sons are killed, pillaged, imprisoned or recruited into a life of crime. Please note that this happens in most communities where poverty and oppression are present, regardless of the race of the people that live in those communities.

Of course, every drug dealer would love to take over the states they live in because this means more money for them, but taking a state involves more military involvement. To better manage the distribution and use of drugs, our government has made selling certain amounts or being caught with a certain amount of drugs a federal crime. This allows the federal government to get involved; this way, a city that cannot afford to take down a drug dealer and his cohorts could rely on state or federal funding. This doesn't mean that drug dealers won't venture outside of their neighborhoods. As a matter of fact, the men and women who sell and distribute drugs in certain territories are what the feds call "small fish in a big pond," meaning, there are people out there who are transporting the drugs from other countries and giving them to these drug dealers; these guys are called drug lords. Drug lords normally create systems where they employ drug traffickers, corrupt city and state officials and distribute large amounts of illegal drugs into certain communities. Wikipedia defines the word "drug lord" this way: "A drug lord, drug baron, kingpin or narco-trafficker is a high-ranking crime boss who controls a sizable network of people involved in the illegal drug trade. Such figures are often difficult to bring to justice, as they are normally not directly in possession of something illegal but are insulated from the actual trade in drugs by several layers of staff. The prosecution of drug lords is therefore usually the result of carefully planned infiltration into their networks, often using informants from within the organization." So, in the natural realm, a drug lord is the spiritual equivalent of a principality. But how do these people come to rule over cities, communities and neighborhoods? Through the power of agreement. Now, please understand there are two types of agreements:

1. **Commonality:** This means to be on one accord with someone. It means to invest money, time, energy or effort into a cause. Another word for this is like-mindedness. In a crime-ridden area, there are people who have no problem with drugs ripping apart their communities. Women who agree will often date, marry or breed with drug dealers, and men who agree will often partner with them or cover for them.

2. **Neutrality:** To be neutral means that you simply refuse to choose a side; you're not for drug dealers, but you're also afraid to go against them. Believe it or not, this is a form of agreement.

Let's briefly discuss neutrality. Remember that a system is like wheels and gears on a machine that's been designed to complete a particular function. In order for some machines to perform certain actions, some of the gears and wheels have to move in the same direction. If any of those particular wheels or gears are moving in the opposite direction, the machine will stall and begin to self-destruct. We understand this. Now, let's image that the wheels are not going in the opposite direction; some wheels and gears are turning clockwise, while the others are simply not moving. They won't move to the left or the right. Can you see how this is just as destructive as the wheels moving in the opposite direction? When the gears from the wheels turning clockwise touch the stalled gears, this will cause them to stall, and consequently, the machine will begin to self-destruct. So, the people who refuse to "snitch" are just as dangerous and destructive as the ones committing the crimes because they are in agreement with the drug dealers through their neutrality. And if the drug dealer is not stopped, he or she will continue to advance, enlarging his or her territory while America turns a blind eye and shifts its attention to the war lords in other nations.

A horizontal boundary is a natural boundary; it's the walls that shape your house, the metal that surrounds your car and it's the direction that you travel in at all times. A vertical boundary, in short, is nothing more than a mindset established by a group of beliefs, experiences and doctrines. "For out of the abundance of the heart the mouth speaketh." (Matthew 12:34). The Lord told us to guard our hearts, for out of it, He says, flows the issues of life. Where does it flow from? Our actions and our mouths. In Matthew 12:34, we find Jesus rebuking the Pharisees, and He then tells them that from out of the abundance of the heart, the mouth speaks. When a man has no boundaries around his heart, his belief system, his tongues and his limbs are hijacked or "leased" by the enemy.

Our horizontal boundaries are determined or predetermined by our vertical ones. For example, many single women (like myself) have decided that we won't allow men in our homes when we're in the courtship phase. This is, of course, a boundary we've established for several reasons, including, but not limited to:

1. Romans 12:1: I beseech you therefore, brethren, by the mercies of God, that ye present your bodies a living sacrifice, holy, acceptable unto God, which is your reasonable service.
2. 1 Thessalonians 5:22: Abstain from all appearance of evil.
3. Romans 12:14:16: Let not then your good be evil spoken of.

This is just one of the vertical boundaries that we've drawn that we have to enforce horizontally, meaning, we can't just plan it in our heads, we have to enforce this with our choices. Will we be pushed, provoked or challenged to lift those boundaries? Of course! Satan wouldn't be Satan if he didn't bother testing us. Nevertheless, if we agree with the Word of God while we are yet still single, and not just think of these boundaries, but publish them in the ears of our leaders, on paper and in public, we are more likely to enforce them than we would if they were just plans. To express a vertical boundary horizontally (in other words, practice what you've planned), you have to take the boundary out of the realm of thought and make it public knowledge. For example, one hundred percent of my single friends who've never officially declared themselves to be abstinent fell into the trap of sexual immorality. They'd joined conversations about abstinence and had even remained untouched for years; this is only because they were single. Nevertheless, the minute they entered into what they believed to be serious relationships, their chastity belts proved to be nothing but aluminum foil. This is why nowadays, I challenge the friends who haven't fallen to study the Word regarding marriage and purity, and to publish their proclamation. Again, this is the power of agreement. Remember, we talked about the three levels or dimensions of the mind, with the conscious mind being the waiting room of the soul. Your proclamation can't be in the waiting room, otherwise, Satan will sit right next to it and begin to dismantle it one lie at a time. He'll play a song that encourages you to sin, send you a friend who encourages you to sin or overwhelm you with a problem that tempts you to sin. And those issues will walk right out of the waiting room and into your subconscious, which is your action/reaction center. From there, your problems will outweigh or outrank your convictions. When this happens, you are more likely to not just sin against God in action (you are not defined by your works), but your sin will be lodged in your heart, meaning, every action that you do is a reaction or response to the condition of your heart. This also means that you'll be in agreement with one or more of the principles belonging to the kingdom of darkness. In other words, you will be a Christian operating in two systems, thus, causing the blessings of God to stall in your life.

- "You're stupid."
- "You're a failure."
- "You'll never be happy."
- "You're not even pretty."
- "God is mad at you!"

These are just a few examples of the lies that Satan says to us; they come vertically and sit in the waiting room of our souls. They can't just move into the subconscious; we have to let them in. To let them in, we have to come into agreement with them. So, if you open your mouth and call yourself stupid, you've just entered into an agreement with Satan. He said that you were stupid, and you agreed with him. And this is what will begin to manifest itself in your life horizontally. This agreement will affect your choices and determine your life's results. This one agreement has the power to dismantle, disrupt and destabilize just about everything in your life.

- "You're blessed and not cursed."
- "You're the head and not the tail."
- "You're the lender and not the borrower."

- "You come behind in no good thing."
- "No weapon that is formed against you shall prosper."

These are the words that fall from Heaven and seat themselves in the waiting rooms of our souls, and many of them have been sitting there for years. Sure, we've memorized them, and we quote them, but we have yet to believe them. Belief takes place in the subconscious mind (short-term) and eventually makes its way to the unconscious mind (long term). How do we pull them down and utilize the benefits of everything God has spoken over us? It's simple. We have to rehearse those words in our heads, publish them with our mouths and write them with our hands. After this, we must act on them. If I say that I'm blessed, I can no longer embrace the cursed mindset of a victim! If I say that I'm the head and not the tail, I have to learn to lead by example. If I say that I'm the lender and not the borrower, I have to work towards being financially independent and refuse to rely on anyone for my substance outside of God. If I say that I come behind in no good thing, I have to stop procrastinating. If I say that no weapon that is formed against me shall prosper, I can't keep running every time Satan releases what appears to be a credible threat against me.

There's power in your agreements. If you agree with God, you'll enter into every season He's appointed you to enter with everything that you need (and want) for that season. But again, your thought life will always express itself in real-time;

this is why it is important (imperative even) for you to take some time to get to know God. Seek Him first, seek Him intently and seek Him consistently. Build your relationship with Him; this way, you won't find yourself being constantly wounded by narcissistic souls simply because you lack boundaries or have trouble enforcing your boundaries. Don't just agree with God in words; maturity happens when you agree with God in the innermost chambers of your heart. When the words of God become the Word of God for you, you have matured! And when the Word of God isn't just a bunch of scriptures but have instead become the laws from which you govern yourself by—this is when your mind is sound enough to respect and understand the boundaries that God has placed around you!

BOUNDARIES IN MARRIAGE

A man lifts his hand to strike his wife for the first time, and with every ounce of force he can muster up, he whips his hand across her face. The force behind the slap causes her to collapse to the ground. Shocked, hurt, angry and confused, she reaches for the left side of her face. She holds her face for a few seconds, trying to make sense of what she's just experienced. Moments later, she lets out a loud shrill as her husband walks away. "I told you to leave it alone, but no! You had to keep on fishing! Now, look at you! Don't cry now!" he shouts as he walks out of their living room and into the kitchen. This isn't the first time he's lost his temper, but in times past, he'd punched the walls in the house and broken a few things, but he'd never hit her up until that moment. The woman stands to her feet, stunned and trying to figure out what she should do. "For better or worse, in sickness and in health, til death do us part." She can hear the sound of their wedding video still playing. She'd been watching the video, trying to get a closer look at one of the women who'd attended her wedding. She'd just discovered that not only was her husband having an affair, but the woman he had been having an affair with had reportedly attended their wedding. She'd discovered this after she'd gone through her husband's phone and found the text message thread between her husband and his mistress. Halfway through the message thread, the mistress wrote,

"Yeah right. It took every ounce of me to stand there and watch you marry someone else, but I didn't want to ruin your big day. I wanted to snatch those flowers from that dingbat and beat her within an inch of her life, but I decided to be nice and snap the pictures." After confronting her husband about the messages, he'd tried to shift the focus from his affair to the fact that his wife had been going through his phone. Not long after that, he'd grabbed his keys and stormed out of their home. Nevertheless, unbeknownst to him, his wife had written down the mistress's phone number, and after he left, she'd plugged the number into Facebook, and a profile popped up. "Wait. Reagan?" She couldn't believe her eyes. She didn't personally know Reagan, but she'd met her a few times at her husband's job, plus, Reagan had been invited to their wedding by her husband. As a matter of fact, Reagan had been one of the photographers at her wedding! Everything was starting to make sense! Hurt, confused and angry, she'd grabbed her phone and sent Reagan a long and ugly text message. Thirty minutes later, her husband stormed through their door, rushed over to his wife and, without warning, struck her. Three years after this event, things between her and her husband still hadn't gotten any better. Instead, every year, he'd grown more and more violent and distant.

Whatever you feed will grow; whatever you starve will die. I've taught this for many years, and in this particular case, the problem is that he's consistently fed his narcissistic desire to control his wife, but this isn't the worst part. The worst part is she's tolerated this, and now, he sees her as a piece of property. Better yet, that Jezebel spirit in him sees her as a piece of property. I've warned both men and women for years on end to walk away from any and every one who dares to physically assault them. The reason behind this isn't centered around teaching the other person a lesson, after all, you cannot domesticate a narcissist. Nothing you do or say will change the way a narcissist sees you or the world. They are broken souls that can only be fixed at the cross of Jesus Christ. Sadly enough, most narcissists do not want to be fixed or rehabilitated. This is because narcissists are oftentimes intelligent creatures who absolutely love controlling and manipulating others because it challenges their intellect, plus, they fear being out of control. Additionally, please note that narcissists rarely feel guilt. Their apologies are centered around themselves; if they do apologize (which is rare), they do so because they are terrified of losing you. This is not because they love you, it's because, once again, they fear not being in control. If the relationship ends, it has to be on their terms. One of the reasons I've passionately told people to run away from their abusive, narcissistic lovers is because narcissists literally grow addicted to the adrenaline and the power they feel every time they strike and dominate another human being. This grows into an insatiable lust that cannot be satisfied, but instead, spreads like a wildfire until it consumes every ounce of their thinking. Of course, Satan is pushing them closer and closer to killing their victims, and if the victim stays, there is a big chance that the narcissist will someday intentionally or unintentionally rob the victim of his/her life.

Marriage, if done God's way, is a beautiful institution where two emotionally and spiritually healthy people unite to create a beautifully mirrored reflection of Christ and His Church. But in order for marriage to even faintly resemble God's original design and purpose for it, both parties in the union must be Christ-like. Please note that being Christ-like is not the same as being Christian. There are some unsaved people out there who are more Christ-like (morally speaking) than many self-professed Christians, and this is why they have healthy, productive marriages. Nevertheless, we live in a time where narcissism and idolatry are both commonplace, so it goes without saying that many of the relationships we see today are as wounded as the folks that are in them. This is why boundaries have to be drawn in marriages, however, the boundaries established in a marriage should only serve to further unite the couple as one person. The two shall be one; we've read this scripture, but do we truly understand what it means? In this text, God is dealing with agreement. Amos 3:3 says, "Can two walk together, except they be agreed?" Agreement is the glue that unites two paths. This doesn't mean that you will agree on everything; it simply means that you should have both personally decided to rank God's will above your own. Therefore, you should both agree to do the will of God; this is what unites the two of you in an agreement, so whenever you disagree about earthly things, you can always turn to the Word of God and settle your dispute. No, the Bible doesn't specifically address many of the issues that arise in marriage by name, but this is because God addresses those issues holistically. For example, He said:

- **Ephesians 5:22-24:** Wives, submit yourselves unto your own husbands, as unto the Lord. For the husband is the head of the wife, even as Christ is the head of the church: and he is the saviour of the body. Therefore as the church is subject unto Christ, so let the wives be to their own husbands in every thing.

- **Ephesians 5:25-33:** Husbands, love your wives, even as Christ also loved the church, and gave himself for it; that he might sanctify and cleanse it with the washing of water by the word, that he might present it to himself a glorious church, not having spot, or wrinkle, or any such thing; but that it should be holy and without blemish. So ought men to love their wives as their own bodies. He that loveth his wife loveth himself. For no man ever yet hated his own flesh; but nourisheth and cherisheth it, even as the Lord the church: For we are members of his body, of his flesh, and of his bones. For this cause shall a man leave his father and mother, and shall be joined unto his wife, and they two shall be one flesh. This is a great mystery: but I speak concerning Christ and the church. Nevertheless let every one of you in particular so love his wife even as himself; and the wife see that she reverence her husband.

- **1 Peter 3:1-6:** Likewise, ye wives, be in subjection to your own husbands; that, if any obey not the word, they also may without the word be won by the conversation of the wives; while they behold your chaste conversation coupled with fear. Whose adorning let it not be that outward adorning of plaiting the hair, and of wearing of gold, or of putting on of apparel; but let it be the hidden man of the heart, in that which is not corruptible, even the ornament of a meek and quiet spirit, which is in the sight of God of great price. For after this manner in the old time the holy women also, who trusted in God, adorned themselves, being in subjection unto their own husbands: Even as Sara obeyed Abraham, calling him lord: whose daughters ye are, as long as ye do well, and are not afraid with any amazement.

- **1 Peter 3:7:** Likewise, ye husbands, dwell with them according to knowledge, giving honour unto the wife, as unto the weaker vessel, and as being heirs together of the grace of life; that your prayers be not hindered.
- **1 Colossians 3:19:** Husbands, love your wives, and be not bitter against them.
- 1 Corinthians 11:3: But I would have you know, that the head of every man is Christ; and the head of the woman is the man; and the head of Christ is God.
- **Proverbs 5:15-20:** Drink waters out of thine own cistern, and running waters out of thine own well. Let thy fountains be dispersed abroad, and rivers of waters in the streets. Let them be only thine own, and not strangers' with thee. Let thy fountain be blessed:

and rejoice with the wife of thy youth. Let her be as the loving hind and pleasant roe; let her breasts satisfy thee at all times; and be thou ravished always with her love. And why wilt thou, my son, be ravished with a strange woman, and embrace the bosom of a stranger?

- **1 Corinthians 7:3-5:** Let the husband render unto the wife due benevolence: and likewise also the wife unto the husband. The wife hath not power of her own body, but the husband: and likewise also the husband hath not power of his own body, but the wife. Defraud ye not one the other, except it be with consent for a time, that ye may give yourselves to fasting and prayer; and come together again, that Satan tempt you not for your incontinency.

Most of the issues that could and would arise in marriage could be resolved holistically using the aforementioned scriptures. All the same, many of the scriptures that are not directly related to marriage can and do solve most marriage-related issues, for example, James 5:12 says, "But above all things, my brethren, swear not, neither by heaven, neither by the earth, neither by any other oath: but let your yea be yea; and your nay, nay; lest ye fall into condemnation." In other words, all of the extra fluff that we add to our words like, "I promise" or "I swear" are unhealthy. This is because they indicate that there is a lack of trust present, therefore, the speaker feels the need to prove himself or herself by ensnaring his or her soul with an oath. To remedy this, the issue of mistrust must be addressed. Does the other spouse have trust issues, and if so, why? Is the speaker trustworthy? Is the speaker a compulsive liar who has a habit of pledging oaths in an attempt to make his/her words more believable? These are issues that must be addressed, not at the surface level, but at the root, meaning, the individual may have to get counseling to get to the bottom of the problem. Nevertheless, the point is, let the Word settle your disputes.

Again, boundaries in marriage should NEVER serve to divide the union; they should be centered around love and respect, both of which help to further unite the couple as one person. Howbeit, it is important to note that any toxic behaviors that go unaddressed will continue to grow and fester until they are big enough to consume the marriage. Let's revisit the abusive husband and his wife. The first time he struck her, the wife should have left. This may seem extreme (to some), but there's a reason behind this that most psychiatrists, psychologists and survivors of abuse can testify to, and that is—tolerating one blow is the same as giving the abuser permission to hit you again. What you do or do not do sends a louder message to your abuser than what you say. This behavior does not and will not stop; that is, unless the victim takes control of his or her own life and removes himself or herself from that equation. This isn't to say that you WHOLEHEARTEDLY must divorce the abusive spouse and that your marriage is doomed; it is to say that if your spouse strikes you, you should remove yourself from that equation until that spouse is repentant AND gets some psychological help. By physically removing yourself from the marital home should a situation like this arise, you are communicating to the spouse that hitting you is NOT okay and will NOT be tolerated EVER! Nevertheless, sticking around communicates the opposite. And it goes without saying that this is a boundary that should have been drawn before the two of you got married, after all, countries don't prepare for war in times of war, they prepare for war in times of peace. Note: It is always better for the victim to remove himself/herself from the marital home because remaining in it means remaining in a place that the controller considers to be his or her domain. If the controller opts to leave instead, he or she is only doing so to ensure that the victim doesn't leave; this allows the controller to maintain a certain measure of control. This also allows the controller to monitor his or her victim. Victims of domestic violence absolutely and without question have to be willing to look foolish, feel foolish and lose whatever they have to lose if they want to win. In other words, they have to be desperate! Jesus said it this way, "For whosoever will save his life shall lose it: and whosoever will lose his life for my sake shall find it" (Matthew 16:25). In all truth, many of us know people who've died trying to hold onto their lifestyles and their reputations while in the face of adversity. We were trying to get them to see the dangers surrounding them, but all they could seem to focus on was what they were losing, how they were feeling and what others were thinking about them. Consequently, they lost the very thing they neglected to place value on and that is their lives.

Another boundary that should be drawn is in regards to the opposite sex. First and foremost, to each his own, just as long as it does not violate the Word of God. With that said, one of the quickest and most effective ways to destroy a marriage is to corrode the trust of one or both of the parties involved. So for example, if your spouse suddenly says that he or she is not comfortable with you having friends of the opposite sex, the best approach to this is to talk with your spouse. Don't argue at the fruit of the issue, look for the root of the issue. For example, find out if one of your friends did something or said something that caused your spouse to feel threatened or uncomfortable. Then again, this may be a personal rule that the spouse entered the marriage with, meaning, the two of you somehow neglected to have that conversation in your haste to say "I do." But speak with the spouse about it, and if he/she is adamant about you not having friends of the opposite sex, honor your spouse's request to keep the peace. This is what God told Abraham to do when Sarah told him to kick Hagar and her son out of their marital home. The Bible tells us that her request grieved Abraham (then Abram), but God told him to hearken (listen) to the voice of his wife. She'd established a boundary; she no longer wanted to share her husband or her home with Hagar, and had Abraham been adamant about keeping his concubine and their son around, he could have lost the promise (Sarah, Isaac) trying to hold onto the counterfeit (Hagar, Ishmael). Most of today's courtrooms are littered with people who've pridefully chosen their egos over their marriages. They left their unions with their pride intact, even though their families (and their hearts) were broken. Note: most of the boundaries or, at least, the major ones, should be or should have been established before you got married. Suddenly telling a spouse about boundaries that he or she was unaware of and did not agree to is selfish, manipulative and divisive. And in cases like these, you can't pencil the boundary into your already established agreements; it has to be discussed, tweaked and agreed upon. What happens if the spouse doesn't agree? What happens if what's important to you is not important to your spouse? The keyword is compromise. Think of it this way—like many other countries, our country has a Constitution; the Constitution is comprised of seven articles written out and agreed upon by America's founding fathers. At that time, America was comprised of 13 states. After the Constitution was drafted, it was sent to each state. It was ratified once nine of the thirteen states had signed the bill. The word "ratify" is defined as "sign or give formal consent to (a treaty, contract, or agreement), making it officially valid" (Source: Google Online Dictionary). The following was taken from WhiteHouse.gov, "A chief aim of the Constitution as drafted by the Convention was to create a government with enough power to act on a national level, but without so much power that fundamental rights would be at risk. One way that this was accomplished was to separate the power of government into three branches, and then to include checks and balances on those powers to assure that no one branch of government gained supremacy. This concern arose largely out of the experience that the delegates had with the King of England and his powerful Parliament. The powers of each branch are enumerated in the Constitution, with powers not assigned to them reserved to the states" (Source: Whitehouse.gov/Our Government/The Constitution).

Let's take what we've learned and apply it to marriage. Marriage is like a country, and both parties involved are citizens of that union. The opposite of a citizen is a stranger or, better yet, a foreigner. A foreigner who commits crimes against the country he or she resides in or is visiting is called a terrorist. Notice the word "terror" in "terrorist." It means extreme fear. So, before we go any further, let's establish the following:

Constitution	Bible
Amendments	What You and Your Spouse Have Agreed to
Citizens	**You and Your Spouse**
Terrorists	Potentially You and Your Spouse

The Constitution of every marriage should be the Word of God. This is where you unite your wills so that they can become one. The amendments are your personal (agreed upon) rules; these are the discussions you had while you were courting. Every agreement after you got married had to be ratified, meaning, both you and your spouse had to agree to the terms before you amended it into your already established Constitution. For example, if your husband said, "I don't want my wife walking around half-dressed," he was telling you a personal rule of his. The moment you said, "I do," that preference became an amendment. You can't marry him and then say, "I never agreed to that." You agreed to marry him knowing that he wanted a wife who dressed modestly. What you could have done, however, was communicate before marriage that you would not comply with his desire to see you dress modestly. If he still decided to marry you, he can't add that clause to the marital contract without your permission. If you sign a contract with a person, you cannot verbally modify the terms within that contract. For example, if I loaned you five hundred dollars and had you to sign a promissory note or a contract agreeing to pay me back the money in full within the next six months (with interest), the moment you sign that contract, you are bound by the terms listed. You cannot call me after the contract has been signed and say, "I've decided that six months is not going to work for me. I'll need eight months at least!" That has no bearing in a U.S. Court of Law. To modify the contract, you'd have to give me something in writing AND I'd have to sign what you gave me agreeing to the terms; the new contract will serve as an amendment. The same is true in marriage. You can't court someone and bait that person into marrying you by agreeing with the individual OR pretending to agree with the individual, only to modify the terms once the two of you have exchanged vows. If a man says that he doesn't want a woman who dresses immoderately, for example, chances are, this isn't the guy for you; that is, unless you're willing to change your mind and your wardrobe. By telling you this, he's letting you know the laws that he governs himself by. When and if the two of you get married, your laws, rules, guidelines and the like will all come together and create a unique set of principles of their own; that is, after you get through the initial turbulence caused by merging your life with that of another human being. However, should you decide to force your spouse to comply with your rules, you are no longer a citizen of that marriage, but a terrorist. Again, the key word is "terror" means "extreme fear." When a spouse starts threatening the other spouse with divorce or separation, that spouse is operating as a terrorist. And one thing to note about terrorists is that they eventually get arrested (bound). After serving their sentences in a federal prison, they are either deported back to their own countries (if they are foreigners) or exiled (if they are citizens). This is the political equivalent of a divorce. This is why it is absolutely important for the parties involved in a relationship to draft up personal amendments and share them with one another BEFORE they get married. It goes without saying that over the course of your marriage, your minds will change and you'll add and remove some amendments, but you can only do this if the two of you agree with the new terms. Write the vision and make it plan; put it on paper and talk about it until you both wholeheartedly understand and agree with the terms. If your spouse does not agree with the new terms, the bill has been vetoed; let it go. This is where your character is further developed. You must learn how to accept the "no" without attempting to punish the person who dared to say it. Trust is built when both parties know that they can disagree respectfully, and the other spouse is not going to "put them on punishment" for not giving in to his or her demands. And again, remember, the Word of God has to be the Supreme Word in your marriage if your marriage going to survive. You cannot and should NEVER place your demands or desires above God's Word. And just like God extends grace to us, we must extend grace to our spouses. It is unrealistic to think that another human being is going to perfectly execute whatever personal amendments we draft up, especially since that same human being cannot perfectly execute following the Word of God. In other words, you have to give your spouse room for error. This is called grace. Again, this builds trust. Trust is paramount in marriage. For example, one of the most eye-opening conversations I've ever had was with a man who'd been married for well over thirty years. He told me that earlier on in their marriage, his wife had come to him and expressed her disdain for a few of the women in his life. Nevertheless, at that time, he felt like she was being insecure and controlling, both of which are poisonous to any marriage. So, he was argumentative and he continued fraternizing with these women because he was determined to prove to her (and himself) that he was the man; he wore the pants! But his wife did something that most women today do not do. She didn't argue with him. She didn't try to press the issue, nor did she put him on punishment for not adhering to her warning. Instead, she gave him the space and the grace to make a decision that was contrary to what she wanted. He said to me, "Tiffany, my wife was right! Every woman, and I do mean EVERY WOMAN that she warned me about ended up being problematic." He told me that a few issues arose in his workplace with some of these women. He didn't tell me the full extent of what happened, but he did say that when the scandals arose, his wife didn't say, "I told you so." He said, "She never once made me feel bad or guilty for not having listened to her. Instead, she took her place beside me and she held my hands up throughout it all." He then went on to say, "This is why I trust that woman with my life!" He ended the story by saying something I'll never forget. He said, "To this day, my wife and I do not argue. We haven't argued in almost thirty years." This guy and his wife have two children, and are successful in just about every area of their lives. He has a successful media company, television show (recorded) and his wife is in the field of medicine. Since I work with ministries, I've had a few conversations like this one, and I noticed the relationship between trust and wealth. When trust is established in a marriage, it ushers in peace, and where there is peace, wealth is inevitable. But trust is first established on the foundation of love and respect. "Nevertheless let every one of you in particular so love his wife even as himself; and the wife see that she reverence her husband" (Ephesians 5:33).

If you're married and the two of you have never drafted up any rules or guidelines, it's not too late to get started. Talk with your spouse about the idea and see what he or she says. If the spouse agrees, great! Whatever you do, just don't start throwing a bunch of unrealistic expectations and demands at your spouse. If your spouse doesn't like the idea, just remember that you can't "draft" it into your marriage. Just make it a point to write down your spouse's complaints and take the time to lovingly, peacefully and respectfully address those complaints, making sure to resolve as many of them as possible. When and if your spouse sees that this is a good system, he or she may be willing to revisit the idea of creating a set of written rules and amendments.

Also, please note that in marriage, people can and do suddenly start introducing problems and demands to the union that were not initially introduced. In situations like these, communication is key! Talk with your spouse, communicate your boundaries, and if the two of you cannot come to an agreement, the best practice is to give the spouse the grace and the space he or she needs to do whatever he or she wants to do; that is, if it's not hurtful or dangerous. The other option is to seek marital counseling. Oftentimes, when a spouse starts operating as a terrorist, there is an underlying issue that needs to be addressed. Ignoring the issue won't make it go away. It'll only grow and fester until it consumes your marriage. And again, I can't say this enough—do NOT tolerate abuse or anything that puts your mind or health at risk. There has to be some boundaries that have a little give to them; then again, there has to be some solid "no's" established. As a reminder, you don't necessarily have to divorce your spouse for breaking one of your solid boundaries, but you should require that he or she gets help for the major issues like abuse (verbal, physical, emotional) and adultery; this is because these issues don't evaporate into thin air. They'll die down for a while, but eventually, they'll gain momentum again, and from there, they will continue to grow. After a while, any toxic behaviors that have been tolerated will become amendments automatically grafted into the fabric of your marriage (compliance equals agreement), and no amount of words, restraining orders or threats will be enough to remedy the issue.

Establish boundaries in marriage; this is important. It is also equally important to respect your spouse's boundaries. Hypocrisy is the assassin of trust. Remember, the objective is to build trust and create a space for you and your spouse to dwell together in absolute peace. And please note that if you are currently in a toxic marriage, and your spouse is not willing to compromise on anything, you may be married to a terrorist. The best practice in this situation is to honor, love, respect and pray for your spouse. You should also communicate your boundaries (no hitting, no cheating, etc.), making it a point to write them down for your spouse to review. From there, put the issue in God's hands. Your new struggle then becomes you having to manage your emotions and overcome the many temptations to "fix your spouse" whenever he or she hurts or disappoints you. Practice holding your peace, but make sure to pray, not just about the issue, but ask God to give you wisdom to navigate the storm you're in. What I've learned over the course of my life is when battling, for example, the narcissist, your best line of defense is SUBMISSION! Most people are terrified of this word, especially when it's paired up with the word "narcissist." Nevertheless, submission is actually a weapon against the enemy. Submission is NOT compliance; it is giving the other person the space and the grace to be as narcissistic and as toxic as he or she wants to be; that is, just as long as the person doesn't engage in dangerous theatrics like becoming physically or emotionally abusive. Understand this—narcissists want control, not submission. People are terrified of the concept of submission because they think it's synonymous with passivity when the two are not even remotely related. Submission deals more with character building than anything; it is the practice of self-control built through self-denial and faith. For example, let's say that your husband suddenly says to you, "I changed my mind. I don't like you having male friends. I don't want Joey calling you anymore." Now, Joey has been your friend for 17 years, and he's never tried to engage you romantically. Nevertheless, for whatever reason, your husband feels threatened by his presence in your life. How should you respond to this? It's simple. Have a talk with Joey, letting him know that your husband is not comfortable with your friendship. Please read this carefully—you are not getting rid of Joey! Chances are, this is just a test and a tantrum from the spouse. Just honor your spouse's request and stop talking to Joey. The problem is NOT with Joey. If your spouse is a narcissist, he's just fishing for control! But when you submit to him instead of fighting with him, his insatiable appetite for control will not be appeased because you are applying a Kingdom method or technology to a demonic issue! Your husband was looking for a fight! Don't give it to him. The worst thing you can say to a narcissist is "Okay," and then follow those words up with, "I love and respect you." Understand that the narcissist came for a fight. When he or she gets love instead, you diffuse the situation by diffusing the person. In a matter of weeks or months, your husband will likely withdraw his petition for you to remove Joey from your life; that is, of course, if Joey isn't problematic. Submission is a weapon of warfare, believe it or not! James 4:7 says, "Submit yourselves therefore to God. Resist the devil, and he will flee from you." The Word tells the wife to reverence her husband and submit to him; by doing this, she is submitting to God. Anytime you submit to God, the enemy has to flee! This doesn't mean he will flee immediately. Chances are, he'll test you, at minimum, three times in one setting before fleeing, after all, this is what he did to Jesus when He was carried into the wilderness by the Spirit to be tempted by the devil. Satan didn't flee the first time Jesus resisted him; he fled the third time. This means that there will be times when you have to consistently fight off his attempts by submitting to God repeatedly. Satan's plan is to wear you down, but God will use the persistence of the enemy to build your faith in Him. Again, the narcissist wants control, not submission! True, God-established submission terrorizes the enemy and is disgusting to the narcissist. Please note that when submitting to a broken soul, you will feel utterly stupid! This is pride manifesting itself, but the more you quench it, the more pride will loosen its grip on you. And when you repeatedly honor, pray for and submit to a narcissist, you are engaging in warfare! You can still communicate your boundaries while submitting.

Take some time out today and create a personal Constitution for yourself. Yes, even if you are unmarried. Write the vision and make it plain, first to yourself, before presenting it to anyone else, and then, to the people closest to you. Establish healthy, realistic boundaries for yourself and others. You'll find that many of the boundaries you've established a long time ago have already been violated because you never formally introduced them to the people in your life. You may have verbally communicated them in passing by saying things like, "I don't like gossipers" or "I couldn't be friends with someone like that," but if you've tolerated gossip, you've amended it into your relationship with that person. Introduce your Constitution to your loved ones, making sure to allow them to make amendments. For example, you can call a friend and say, "I created a new Constitution for myself and it's amazing! I think you should create one as well! I'll show you mine whenever you have time." When you do show her (or him) your Constitution, you'll be able to go over the laws that you plan to govern your life by. So, you can say, "No gossiping for any reason." You can explain each rule or law as you go along. All the same, encourage all of your loved ones to create their own personal Constitutions so that you can make amendments. (Please note that they do not have to sign these Constitutions; they are simply designed to help you govern yourself.) And if you're married, speak with your spouse about coming together so that the two of you can create the laws that govern your behaviors and conversations in marriage. If he or she refuses, create your own and present it to the spouse; this personal Constitution of yours should list what you will and will not do, along with what you will and will not say. For example, in my personal Constitution, one of my rules is, "I will not walk away from any covenant relationships. Whenever I'm offended or hurt, I will pray about the issue, wrestle down my own emotions, and if needed, I will communicate with the person I'm offended with or hurt by. I will only walk away if the person is not willing to resolve the issue, thus causing the relationship to become toxic, unhealthy and ungodly. Even in that, I'd be prayerful! I may take my distance but not necessarily renounce my relationship with the person; that is, until I know for sure that God is clearing me to walk away. In short, this is the commitment I've made to fight for my covenant relationships, as difficult as it may be at times. When your spouse sees you honoring, first the Word of God, and next, what you've lined out in your Constitution, he or she may want to create his or her own. All the same, by you respecting your own boundaries, you teach your spouse (and others) to respect your boundaries. And it goes without saying that before you can draft up a covenant Constitution and enforce it, you first need to draft up a personal Constitution and use it as a tool of self-governance. For example, you have to master self-control; that is, you have to master loving people, forgiving people and above all, just honoring the Word of God—consistently and habitually! Trying to draft up a covenant Constitution when you don't have or honor your own personal Constitution is a mechanism of control; it's manipulative and unhealthy. You have to discipline yourself first, and then, when you're mature and healthy enough to introduce this concept to the people in your life, it can and will prove to be invaluable. But in the meantime, draft up one for yourself and master it.

Marriage is beautiful when it's done God's way. But because the people involved are wrapped in flesh, they are prone to error, and whatever issues God has with them are the same issues you will have with them. This is why God drew boundaries around Himself and everything that He renders to be holy; of course, this teaches us to do the same, even in marriage.

Genesis 3:22-24: And the LORD God said, Behold, the man is become as one of us, to know good and evil: and now, lest he put forth his hand, and take also of the tree of life, and eat, and live for ever: Therefore the LORD God sent him forth from the garden of Eden, to till the ground from whence he was taken. So he drove out the man; and he placed at the east of the garden of Eden Cherubims, and a flaming sword which turned every way, to keep the way of the tree of life.

UNDERSTANDING CRIMES

Luke 1:5-23: There was in the days of Herod, the king of Judaea, a certain priest named Zacharias, of the course of Abia: and his wife was of the daughters of Aaron, and her name was Elisabeth. And they were both righteous before God, walking in all the commandments and ordinances of the Lord blameless. And they had no child, because that Elisabeth was barren, and they both were now well stricken in years.

And it came to pass, that while he executed the priest's office before God in the order of his course, according to the custom of the priest's office, his lot was to burn incense when he went into the temple of the Lord. And the whole multitude of the people were praying without at the time of incense. And there appeared unto him an angel of the Lord standing on the right side of the altar of incense. And when Zacharias saw him, he was troubled, and fear fell upon him. But the angel said unto him, Fear not, Zacharias: for thy prayer is heard; and thy wife Elisabeth shall bear thee a son, and thou shalt call his name John. And thou shalt have joy and gladness; and many shall rejoice at his birth. For he shall be great in the sight of the Lord, and shall drink neither wine nor strong drink; and he shall be filled with the Holy Ghost, even from his mother's womb. And many of the children of Israel shall he turn to the Lord their God. And he shall go before him in the spirit and power of Elias, to turn the hearts of the fathers to the children, and the disobedient to the wisdom of the just; to make ready a people prepared for the Lord. And Zacharias said unto the angel, Whereby shall I know this? For I am an old man, and my wife well stricken in years. And the angel answering said unto him, I am Gabriel, that stand in the presence of God; and am sent to speak unto thee, and to shew thee these glad tidings. And, behold, thou shalt be dumb, and not able to speak, until the day that these things shall be performed, because thou believest not my words, which shall be fulfilled in their season.

And the people waited for Zacharias, and marvelled that he tarried so long in the temple. And when he came out, he could not speak unto them: and they perceived that he had seen a vision in the temple: for he beckoned unto them, and remained speechless. And it came to pass, that, as soon as the days of his ministration were accomplished, he departed to his own house.

As you can see, Zacharias crossed a boundary; this is the boundary of doubt. Whenever God gives you instructions, you will find yourself at a crossroads. To your left, you'll see logic and every reasonable explanation as to why you shouldn't believe God. To your right, you'll see what God said, but God doesn't explain His instructions to us often. He just tells us to obey. Of course, He does this to grow our trust in Him. Zacharias chose to go left instead of right. Because of this, he had to deal with a measure of bondage; he had to suffer through a limitation, and get this, the angel said that he would remain dumb until the prophecy came to pass. This means that Zacharias, like any other prisoner, had been sentenced to spend a certain amount of time in bondage. What I've come to learn about bondage is, most people serve time in certain seasons because they crossed a boundary that they weren't supposed to cross, or they allowed people to cross boundaries in their lives that they were supposed to protect.

"I sentenced you to five years in that marriage because you would not hearken to my voice!" *Sentenced.* What a strong word, but amazingly enough, many believers to this date are "serving time" in toxic relationships because of rebellion or doubt. The cuffs that hold them to their broken, narcissistic lovers is called a yoke or, better yet, a soul tie. I've lost count of the many times women have reached out to me, complaining about being married to narcissists. Of course, they'd tried to take a shortcut to their blessings, opting to sin their way into marriage, only to find themselves soul-tied to Satan's favorite weapon—Jezebel. Of course, those women were trying to find legal ways out of their marriages, not realizing that there is a lesson in (some of) those marriages that God wants them to get. So, if they "escape" before He releases them, they are likely to end up dating and marrying that same demon in a different man. Divorce statistics prove this. And why would this happen? Because they haven't gotten the revelation they needed to get free and remain free. Therefore, they'd leave their marriages prematurely and they'd blame the failure of the marriage on the husband. No circle or cycle is complete until you get back to the starting point, meaning, the evidence of their immaturity is found in the fact that they will not take accountability for their wrongs. "He cheated on me, he was a compulsive liar, he manipulated me, and he refused to get a job." A complaint such as this one seems to be a plausible argument for divorce, however, he was a manipulative liar and cheater when she'd decided to sin against God to secure her relationship with him. None of those complaints were plausible enough to keep her from marrying him, but the minute she realizes that he loves being the way he is, she starts running towards the border, hoping to free herself. The problem with this is three-fold:

1. **She hasn't gotten the wisdom out of the situation.** What should she get from this? That the Word of God is true; that's the key! She doubted God and believed that she could unequally yoke herself with an unbeliever, even though the Bible warns us not to. She believed that a house divided could stand after all, even though the Word says otherwise. She didn't believe that she'd reap what she'd sown, because she was more focused on her intentions than she was on her seeds. She didn't believe that she needed to present her body as a living sacrifice, holy and acceptable to God, which was her reasonable service. So, if she runs when she has accepted that the Word is true, she'll blame the guy for the failure of the relationship, focusing on the fruits; that is, the issues that sprouted up in that relationship, rather than

106

focusing on the seeds sown.

2. **She hasn't found herself in the equation.** No season is complete until we can take accountability for our own wrongs. Blame is deflecting. Sure, her husband may have been an abusive cheater; in short, he's a wild animal. But she has to admit that she captured him in the wilderness, gave the sin offering and tried to force God into accepting a demon-bound man who had no desire to be free.

3. **God still isn't first in her life.** Matthew 6:33 reads, "But seek ye first the kingdom of God, and his righteousness; and all these things shall be added unto you." Our job is to chase the Kingdom of God, but she did like most believers. She's been so focused on her husband and all the pain he's brought into her life that she hasn't had the time or the desire to pursue God. She has been pursuing His hands though, just not His heart.

This could only mean that if God were to provide her with the way of escape, she'd escape her marriage still seeing herself as the victim, not realizing that she too is a predator. How so? There are two kingdom dynamics; there is the Kingdom of God and then there is the kingdom of darkness. When a believer goes after an unbeliever, both parties are both promoted and demoted, depending on the kingdom they are settled in. Think of it this way—Ahab was king over northern Israel; he ruled that section of the world, but when he stepped foot in Phoenicia, he had absolutely no jurisdiction.

He was still king over northern Israel, but when he went to shake hands with Ishbaal (Jezebel's father) and to pick up his new bride, he was at King Ishbaal's mercy. But if ever and whenever Ishbaal came to Israel, he initially had no jurisdiction; that is, until Ahab entered into an agreement with the Phoenician government in exchange for their protection. What does this mean? Let's revisit the saved woman versus unsaved narcissistic guy dynamic. In the church, the guy will be seen as the predator; this is because he is unsaved, double-minded or immature, and he is wreaking havoc in his marriage. This, of course, means that his wife will be seen as the prey. In the world, on the other hand, the woman will be seen as the predator because she's trying to keep her husband from doing what he normally does, she's constantly arguing with him and she's allowing the church to destroy their relationship. But there's another dynamic that we have yet to consider. That's the Kingdom dynamic, not the church's. In the Kingdom, the real predator is the believer. How so? Because she was sleeping with someone who's either not born again or someone who's immature in the faith, which would make her a spiritual pedophile. Think of what this looks like in the natural. Imagine that a female teacher started having a relationship with one of her 13-year old students. The woman is 26-years old. She manages to get away with it, and on his 18th birthday, the couple elope, to his parents' horror. Two years later, the woman takes her now estranged husband to court. He wants to go to college and finally start his life, but his estranged wife is angry, bitter and determined to destroy his life. "Your honor, he has two sons to take care of!" she yells in her New York accent. His mother stands alongside him and pleads with the judge for mercy. "My son isn't working right now. He hasn't gone to college because his seventh-grade teacher decided to rape him and steal his childhood away from him. She made him get fired from the pizzeria that he was working at, and now, she's suing him for back child support. Your Honor, she's doing everything in her might to keep him from going to college. Yes, he's immature, but what 18-year old boy isn't?" The judge is almost ready to render her verdict when the estranged wife speaks up again. "Your Honor, this man cheated on me, he couldn't keep a job and all he wanted to do was play with his PlayStation all day long! He needs to be held accountable! He was grown when we got married, so I don't know why his mother is complaining!" If you were the judge in this scenario, who would you rule in favor of? Most people would rule in favor of the young man, after all, he was simply acting his age. The teacher had a responsibility to teach him; that's it and that's all. Instead, she crossed several boundaries when she decided to groom him to be her lover and ultimately her husband. And while he may have looked mature, the truth is, he was a child! This is how God sees it whenever we cross boundaries and unequally yoke ourselves with people who have not been ushered into the Kingdom yet or people who are babes in Christ. "But whoever causes one of these little ones who believe in Me to sin, it would be better for him if a millstone were hung around his neck, and he were drowned in the depth of the sea" (Matthew 18:6). The point is that we can't focus on what grows in our gardens more than we focus on what we planted in our gardens. If your garden is filled with weeds and you cut them down, they'll keep growing back up until you deal with the root of the issue. Again, this why most people who tend to attract narcissists often find themselves dating one narcissist behind the other. This isn't to blame the victim; it is to educate and empower those who see themselves as victims; this way, they can:

1. Take accountability. This is what opens the door to the next season.
2. Walk in victory. Victimhood is a neighborhood of thinking that can only be escaped when a person decides not to be a victim anymore.

Let's revisit the example of a woman in a toxic marriage. The sound of a soul tie interrupts her silence. She falls on her face and tries to drag herself out of that marriage, but she can't leave just yet. Something is holding her back. So, she lowers her head and begins to plead with God. She's being tormented and she wants it to stop. She lifts her head and tries to get through another day, but her narcissistic husband seems to be getting worse. He keeps crossing boundaries that she's put in place to protect their marriage and her sanity, and the more he does this, the more toxic and arrogant he becomes. "Be quiet and know that I am God." This is the only instruction God seems to give to her in her darkest hour. How do you be still when everything in you and around you is collapsing? And the more she tries to be still, the more her husband violates her boundaries. At the edge of her sanity, she calls on the name of the Lord again, but He doesn't answer. "Maybe God is mad at me," she reasons with herself, but this is not true. She'd crossed a boundary when she'd unequally yoked herself with an unbeliever, and she'd crossed another boundary when she'd decided to give her body as a living sacrifice, unholy and unacceptable to God because she was too busy lying down with a demonic principal. Her pillow begins to deteriorate because of her many tears and her voice begins to deepen because of all the yelling. She wants out of the marriage, but why won't God set her free? It's simple. Because there's wisdom, knowledge, understanding and answers there that she has not yet embraced. Better yet, she hasn't grown. Again, should God release her early; yes, even for good behavior, she'd end up marrying the same devil in a different man. She'd end up sinning to get another guy, reasoning within herself that there was simply something wrong with her ex. So, she ends up serving a sentence that is designed to make her pray more, pray harder and pray longer. There's a penalty for rebellion, even though many believers want to believe that the system of sowing and reaping is now obsolete. It isn't. It's still as potent today as it was thousands of years ago. Nothing God says loses its momentum or its power ... ever!

I remember being a young girl when I went with my parents and siblings to visit one of my uncles. He was in prison. I'm not sure what crime or crimes he'd committed, but what I do remember is that he spent a large part of his life behind bars.

He was paying the price for his sins against humanity, whether that sin had been robbing a bank or selling drugs. They took us on the yard to see him, and I remember how proud he seemed to be that he was locked up. He made his way over to us and began speaking as if he'd arrived in life; it was as if he was advising us on how to become another version of himself. Looking at my brother, I could tell that he was buying into the lie. His eyes lit up as my uncle straddled over a bench, sat down and began to speak with so much confidence. To my brother, he was like a celebrity; to my brother, he was everything that he'd wanted to become: bold, articulate, confident and unmoved by societal norms.

When we left the prison that day, I looked over at my brother. We were in the backseat of our parents' car, and he was quieter than normal. What's worse was, he had a smug look on his face; it was almost as if he was fantasizing about the experience he'd just had. I was about eleven or twelve-years old and I wanted to shatter whatever thoughts my brother had in his head. I don't remember the exact words that I spoke, but I do remember saying something to my brother, and he responded with, "Bet." That was my uncle's favorite closing statement; I'd never heard my brother say that word before that moment, but he'd just been in the presence of his idol, and it was clear to me that he had set his sights on what he'd wanted to become. I tried to convince my brother to go in another direction, but being a young lady, I didn't know how to articulate it in a way that he'd understand, so I tried mocking him. "Stop trying to be like Uncle Joseph!" I shouted. *Of course, Joseph isn't his actual name; I'm using that name for anonymity.* My brother looked straight up ahead and responded; this was another one of my uncle's nuances—he would slightly lift his head in a proud way whenever he was offended, refusing to look at his offender. This was normally my uncle's way of issuing a threat. Of course, this was something he'd seen on television and began to mimic. "I'm not trying to be like Uncle Joseph," he said, smacking his lips and turning to look out the passenger's window. I got even more upset. "You are not Uncle Joseph! I don't know why you think that's cute!" From there, we argued and our parents threatened to punish us if we didn't stop, so we did. From that day forth, my brother continued to pattern himself after my uncle. When my uncle was released from prison, he came to stay with us for a brief stint. Howbeit, he was a bound man, so wherever he laid his head, he'd lay everything that was in his head, including his women. My uncle would bring, at minimum, three different women to our house every week to sleep with. What surprised me the most was the fact that my parents allowed this. That was, until the women started randomly showing up at our house and catching him with other women. From there, a fight would ensue, and the police would be called. After a few brawls in our driveway, my parents decided to set some boundaries in our home. When they did this, my uncle moved out of the house. He could not and would not live anywhere where boundaries had been established, especially if those boundaries were being enforced. My brother, on the other hand, would grow up and continue patterning himself after my uncle until he one day realized that there was nothing cute about repeatedly listening to the sounds of a judge's gavel.

My uncle's sins against mankind had price tags attached to them, some that he would often elude for short spaces of time. One thing I learned about sin is that it always comes to collect its wages. *Always.* My uncle's sins against God had price tags attached to them, some that he would often seem to elude for short and extended spaces of time, but the system of sowing and reaping is absolute. It cannot and will not fail. So, it goes without saying, I saw what crime did to my uncle naturally, just as I saw what sin did to him spiritually.

Penalties. Every crime has penalties attached to it. There is a minimum penalty and a maximum penalty for every (legal) crime. Please note that the word "crime" is just the secular version of the word "sin." And just as every crime has penalties attached to it, every sin has penalties attached to it. For example, here are a few crimes and penalties under Georgia State law.

Crime	Definition	Punishment
Murder	A homicide committed with malice aforethought (that is, the murderer	Death or life imprisonment

Crime	Definition	Punishment
	planned or intended to kill the victim).	
Voluntary Manslaughter	A homicide committed when the person acts as the result of a "sudden, violent, and irresistible passion" resulting from provocation sufficient to cause it (for example, a homicide resulting from a family quarrel).	1 - 20 years
Involuntary Manslaughter	A homicide committed unintentionally while committing an unlawful act other than a felony (for example, a homicide accidentally resulting from someone firing a	1-10 years

As misdemeanor** |

Crime	Definition	Punishment
	gun in the city limits, a misdemeanor). OR a homicide committed unintentionally by committing a lawful act in an unlawful manner likely to cause death or serious bodily harm.	
Kidnapping	The abducting or stealing away of any person without lawful authority and the holding of that person against his or her will. Kidnapping a person for ransom or injuring the person kidnapped.	10-20 Years Life imprisonment
Aggravated Assault	Assault with intent to murder, rape, or rob with a deadly weapon.	1-20 years 3-20 years

Crime	Definition	Punishment
	If victim is 65 or over.	5-20 years
	If victim is a police officer.	
Treason (State Level)	A breach of one's duty of allegiance to one's state or country. Levying war against the state or country or giving aid or comfort to the enemies of the state or country.	15 years - life imprisonment
Armed Robbery	Taking the property of another when the offender uses a weapon.	10-20 years or life imprisonment

You'll notice that every time the news reports on someone being arrested for a crime, they always finish the story with, "If found guilty, the assailant could spend up to ____ years in prison." This, of course, is done to discourage copycat criminals from doing what they do best—copying! News anchors know that any and every time a crime is reported, there is some bound, twisted individual who will be inspired to commit the same type of crime. What's been keeping these people from following through with their sick and twisted fantasies over the years? Fear. They are afraid of being caught and afraid of going to prison. So, they sit around their homes and fantasize about causing minor to widespread devastation. And when they see someone else who thinks and reasons like them carrying out their fantasies, in that moment, fear seems to dissipate. In that moment, what we see as the photo of a crazed criminal, they see as the photo of a genius—someone to idolize. And if their thoughts are not immediately addressed and dismantled, they'll go out and commit copycat crimes. To keep this from happening, news anchors and other media outlets often report on the maximum penalties that the criminal is facing. And while this isn't one hundred percent effective, it has proven to be, at minimum, ninety percent effective. There are more criminals or, better yet, demonized people living around us than we care to know.

Let's go back to the saved woman with the unsaved man. When she crossed the boundary of sin to get her man, she was already bound, but she entered further and further into bondage. When she brought her guy into the church, he was already bound, but he entered further and further into bondage, thus, their house began to split. But wait! Isn't the church supposed to set him free? No. This is a finished work of Jesus Christ. He has to want to be free; deliverance is not a magic spell. It's a choice. All the same, whenever and if ever she decides to run out of the marriage, she may find herself unable to break free of his "power." In truth, this isn't an actual power; it's a soul tie. Another word for "soul tie" is "yoke." So, when God said for us to refrain from unequally yoking ourselves with unbelievers, He was simply telling us to not soul tie ourselves to them in a manner where we'd have to share a load with them. But a soul tie can and does double as a zip tie or a cord of bondage whenever it's used to tie people together from opposing kingdoms. And cry as she may, the woman in question may find herself "sentenced" to several seasons with the guy; that is, until she finally repents and agrees with God. Now, God didn't put her in the relationship to punish her, after all, He didn't put her in the relationship at all! He simply didn't break the soul tie between the woman and her choice. He allowed her to reap what she'd sown. This was so that should she be single again, she'd realize that she is royalty and would therefore refuse to date or marry any guy she met in her wilderness season.

SOWING AND REAPING

Imagine this—you purchase a gift basket for your neighbor who lives ten minutes away from you. You then hand that gift basket to your 15-year old son and ask him to deliver it to the neighbor. The problem is, there are two ways to get to your neighbor's house—there's a shortcut through a field, but it's not the safest route to take. It would, however, save your son five minutes going and five minutes returning. The other route is the traditional sidewalk route. Of course, you tell your son to avoid the wilderness path, after all, there's no telling what he would encounter while walking through the field. Nevertheless, like most 15-year old boys, he wants to take the easy route, especially since you interrupted him playing one of his favorite video games. It goes without saying that he doesn't heed your warning. He rushes off into the field, hoping that you haven't noticed the path he's decided to take. While in the field, he experiences a few insect bites, but in his mind, this is a small price to pay to save himself some time. In the distance, he notices a puddle. Unfortunately, there's no way around it. To the left of the puddle is extremely tall grass, thorns and bushes; to the right of the puddle, there's extremely tall grass, thorns and bushes. He'd completely lose himself if he were to walk into the grass, so he has to make a difficult decision; he has to walk through the puddle. He finally arrives at the puddle, and like any normal human being, he studies the puddle to get an idea as to how deep it is. A few feet away, he finds a stick and sticks it in the puddle. It would cover his ankles, meaning, his shoes would be ruined, but there's no turning back now. He's been on the path for three minutes, with two minutes left on his route. He places one foot in the puddle. It's cold, sticky and extremely unpleasant. Nevertheless, he decides to continue through the puddle, and just when he finally reaches the edge of it, he stumbles and falls. Thankfully, the basket doesn't fall into the puddle. It suffers some slight, nearly unnoticeable damage, and the only thing hurt on your son is his pride. He stands to his feet, picks the basket back up and continues on his journey. Two minutes later, he finally arrives at the neighbor's house. He knocks on the door, and the neighbor's 14-year old son answers the door. "Hey, my Mom told me to bring this basket over. Is Mrs. Margaret home?" The 14-year old considers letting the young man in, but once he sees the mud on his pants and the lower part of his shirt, he decides against it, knowing that his mother would panic if she saw the young man standing in her living room. "I'll take it," he says. And with that, the young man grabs the basket and notifies his mother who tells him to bring it to her. The 15-year old rebel is now ready to return to his house, but the problem is, he has a decision to make. He could go back down that unpredictable path and go back through the mud puddle or he could go the long route. Being 15-years old and impatient, he chooses to take the shortcut again. And this time, he meets another issue on the way. Just a minute before reaching his house, he sees movement in the grass right at the edge of the path. He suddenly freezes, hoping that whatever it is will go away or, at minimum, it's a raccoon or something that's relatively harmless. The grass shakes for more than seven minutes, while the young man stands still, waiting for his opportunity to at least run the rest of the way to his house, after all, he could see his home in the distance. But all of a sudden, the creature makes itself known. It's a small alligator! Obviously, there's a swamp nearby. Suddenly, the young man turns around and runs in the opposite direction. A minute later, he runs through the puddle and stumbles again, this time, halfway through the puddle. Covered in mud, he leaps to his feet and runs until he's out of the field. Once safely out of the field, he reasons within himself that he will never walk through that field again. He then starts his five-minute journey towards his house using the path his mother told him to use.

This story is designed to teach a moral lesson. First and foremost, we all want something that seems to be far away and outside of our reach. But to keep us from taking the wrong paths to get to what we want, God told us to be anxious for nothing; this includes marriage and money! Nevertheless, most of us don't heed the warning. Like the 15-year old young man, we look for shortcuts to get to whatever it is we've been fantasizing about. And those shortcuts are off the beaten paths that Christ carved out for us. Howbeit, they look safe enough. As a matter of fact, most believers are on these paths chasing their dreams (and their exes). And it doesn't matter how many people we see running back towards Christ to take the right route, we still reason within our minds that our stories won't look like theirs. So, off we go into the wilderness, fantasizing about the moment that we'll emerge from the jungle unscathed, married, rich, happy and radiant. Instead, when we finally do emerge some years later, we come out holding restraining orders, divorce papers and child support orders. These are what we call penalties. Oxford Language defines the word "penalty" as: "a punishment imposed for breaking a law, rule, or contract." What rules did we break? Below, you'll find a few of our crimes:

1. Romans 12:1: I beseech you therefore, brethren, by the mercies of God, that ye present your bodies a living sacrifice, holy, acceptable unto God, which is your reasonable service.
2. 2 Corinthians 6:14: Be ye not unequally yoked together with unbelievers: for what fellowship hath righteousness with unrighteousness? And what communion hath light with darkness?
3. 2 Corinthians 6:17: Wherefore come out from among them, and be ye separate, saith the Lord, and touch not the unclean thing; and I will receive you.
4. Matthew 6:33: But seek ye first the kingdom of God, and his righteousness; and all these things shall be added unto you.
5. Mark 12:30: And thou shalt love the Lord thy God with all thy heart, and with all thy soul, and with all thy mind, and with all thy strength: this is the first commandment.

6. 2 Corinthians 10:5: Casting down imaginations, and every high thing that exalteth itself against the knowledge of God, and bringing into captivity every thought to the obedience of Christ.
7. Exodus 20:3: Thou shalt have no other gods before me.

And this is just a short list! Amazingly enough, you'll find the word "pen" in the words "penalties" and "repentance." This is because we get to write the script that is our lives. Whatever we pencil into our stories will determine how our stories end. Nevertheless, we live in a time and a culture where the word "repent" is now viewed negatively by both believers and unbelievers alike; this is because most people associate this word with judgment. Howbeit, when David was confronted by the Prophet Nathan about his sins and crimes against Uriah, he readily repented. David knew he was wrong all along, but like many men and women in power, he'd likely became lifted up in his heart. Let's look at this confrontation.

2 Corinthians 12:1-15 (ESV): And the Lord sent Nathan to David. He came to him and said to him, "There were two men in a certain city, the one rich and the other poor. The rich man had very many flocks and herds, but the poor man had nothing but one little ewe lamb, which he had bought. And he brought it up, and it grew up with him and with his children. It used to eat of his morsel and drink from his cup and lie in his arms, and it was like a daughter to him. Now there came a traveler to the rich man, and he was unwilling to take one of his own flock or herd to prepare for the guest who had come to him, but he took the poor man's lamb and prepared it for the man who had come to him." Then David's anger was greatly kindled against the man, and he said to Nathan, "As the Lord lives, the man who has done this deserves to die, and he shall restore the lamb fourfold, because he did this thing, and because he had no pity." Nathan said to David, "You are the man! Thus says the Lord, the God of Israel, 'I anointed you king over Israel, and I delivered you out of the hand of Saul. And I gave you your master's house and your master's wives into your arms and gave you the house of Israel and of Judah. And if this were too little, I would add to you as much more. Why have you despised the word of the Lord, to do what is evil in his sight? You have struck down Uriah the Hittite with the sword and have taken his wife to be your wife and have killed him with the sword of the Ammonites. Now therefore the sword shall never depart from your house, because you have despised me and have taken the wife of Uriah the Hittite to be your wife.' Thus says the Lord, 'Behold, I will raise up evil against you out of your own house. And I will take your wives before your eyes and give them to your neighbor, and he shall lie with your wives in the sight of this sun. For you did it secretly, but I will do this thing before all Israel and before the sun.'" David said to Nathan, "I have sinned against the Lord." And Nathan said to David, "The Lord also has put away your sin; you shall not die. Nevertheless, because by this deed you have utterly scorned the Lord, the child who is born to you shall die." Then Nathan went to his house.

Notice that God said David had despised Him. Why had He said this? The truth is, anytime we rebel against the Word of the Lord, we are rebelling against God, Himself. We cannot separate God from His Word because He is His Word, and His Word is Lord! And because of David's sins against God, he paid a pretty hefty price. Again, this is called a penalty. In truth, we understand and agree with penalties as it relates to our criminal justice system, but the average believer sees spiritual penalties as cruel and unnecessary. Consequently, there are a lot of people out and about who are angry with God, not because of what He's done, but because their sins didn't bear fruit for them in the Kingdom. Read that again! People sow seeds in the kingdom of darkness and then look for their harvests in God's Kingdom, and this is simply not how it works! In truth, we've learned to humanize God and even attempt to make Him serve us. We often look at our intentions, rather than focusing on the fact that we are breaking God's ordinances. "I know we're not married yet, but we plan to get married so I don't think that what we're doing is that big of a deal when there are rapists and killers out there." Many believers living in sexual sin either say this aloud or they, at minimum, reason like this in their minds! This is the created telling the Creator what He should and should not be focusing on. Consequently, many believers end up in relationships with the weapons that were formed against them, and when those relationships don't prosper, they blame God. This is what it means to despise Him. It means that the only way we'll honor Him is if He goes against His very nature to let us have what we want AND He

127

must also control the people we sin with and make them play into our fantasies! We have to see what this looks like on paper; this way, we can stop playing the victims or being the victims. This way, we can pencil in a different choice—one that allows God to bless, prosper and use us, but first, we have to repent.

Repentance

"Repent! For the Kingdom of God is at hand!" John, the Baptist's words have echoed over the centuries and are still as loud today as they were the day he said them. Nevertheless, many of today's Christians are trying to drown out this sound with any and everything they can find. What I've observed over the years is that many believers who are immature or rebellious (double-minded) will steer clear of anyone who promotes holiness and repentance. Instead, they'd prefer to hear about grace because, for many believers, grace, to them, is nothing but a condom designed to help them enter and enjoy the pleasures of sin without having to endure the consequences of sin. But just as there is a hole in their logic, there is a hole in this proverbial condom. You see, grace was never intended to be abused. God did not extend grace to the believer as a license to sin against Him. As a matter of fact, the Greek word for "grace" is "charis" ad it means: "(a) grace, as a gift or blessing brought to man by Jesus Christ, (b) favor, (c) gratitude, thanks, (d) a favor, kindness" (Source: Strong's Concordance). What's funny is, we often tell people, "Don't take my kindness for my weakness!" In other words, don't abuse the grace I extend to you, because we know people who will do just that—abuse it! All the same, people who are known to stiffen their necks and squint their eyes at others before parroting these same words are the main ones who take God's grace for granted! When the woman who was caught in the very act of adultery had been pardoned by Jesus, He'd stopped her accusers from stoning her to death. In other words, He gave her the space and the grace to repent! What did He say to her? Did He tell her to just ignore the guys; did He tell her that they were just a bunch of religious haters who needed to mind their own business? No! He told her to go away and sin no more! This means that Jesus rebuked her too, but He rebuked her according to her age, meaning He was soft with her, but hard on her accusers. Again, He told her to repent. Please note that the word "repent" means to turn away from a particular sin; it means to change directions. To repent isn't to apologize, even though apologizing is an expression or declaration that we make when we are repenting. In other words, apologizing is an extension of repentance, but it's not the fullness of repentance. To repent means to turn all the way back and begin to work or walk with God again; it means to agree with God and to intentionally do His will, even when your flesh wants to do otherwise.

Why does God call us to repentance? Because He loves us. The answer is simple, even though we often complicate it because our human logic won't allow us to understand the whys, the whats and the hows behind God's Word. If it doesn't make sense to us, we often place it in the waiting room of our minds for years on end, which means that we are filled with more human logic than we are with the Word of God. This imbalance causes us to be carnal; it also provokes us to become angry with God whenever one plus one in the natural does not equate to two in the spirit. God calls every single one of us to repentance because He wants to bless us, He wants to use us, and He wants to prosper us. Nevertheless, if we are partaking in two systems (the Kingdom of God and the kingdom of darkness), there's no possible way for us to be blessed. Sure, God can give us His grace and His mercy, but sometimes, He has to draw back the boundaries on His mercy, allowing the enemy that we've been serving to violently remind us that there are no blessings in sin, neither is sin a shortcut to a blessing. For example, we see it all the time. A woman who's been Christian and single for a long time gets tired of being single. She finally meets a guy and they start a relationship. Worried that the man won't marry her if she doesn't give him a sin offering, she ends up having sex with the guy. And she does this repeatedly, thinking that the two of them love one another, so they'll be getting married anyway. So, she pushes back the boundaries on her perspective, not realizing that anytime you lift the boundaries that God has placed around your purity and sexuality, perversion will begin to advance in your life. It seems to work. One day, the man gets on one knee and utters the words she's been longing to hear. "Will you marry me?" Tears weld up in her eyes as onlookers begin to applaud, not realizing what she's about to say, "I do" to. She plans a nice wedding and she makes sin look good. Because of this, many people begin to reason within themselves that sexual purity isn't so necessary after all. But God has to back His Word! The couple stand on the altar in front of a pastor, agreeing to be living examples of what not to do. "I do," they say, staring one another in the eyes, marrying their imaginations of one another, not realizing that soberness is just a few months down the road, and he's got a reality check in the passenger's seat.

"He's addicted to porn." Her words are followed by complete silence, and then the agonizing sounds of her heart breaking all the more. Her voice quivers as she speaks. "And I can't take it anymore." What she hadn't realized was that, she had been feeding his perversion the whole time. This is like a high interest loan. Paying the minimum balance only addresses the interest, but it doesn't touch the loan. The same is true for her. She finds herself having sex with her husband, only to realize that during the entirety of their relationship, she's been touching his perversion and not his heart; she has yet to touch (or meet) the man himself because perversion has him in captivity. Sure, she's given into these carnal desires, she's looked him in the eyes, and she's had countless heart-to-heart conversations with him, but she lived in his conscious mind because there was no room for her in his subconscious. Perversion lived in his subconscious, and from there, it had managed to place him in solitary confinement. He called it introversion, but the truth was, in his case, he was just too ashamed to be around people because guilt had stolen every ounce of his confidence. All the same, perversion wore a bigger ring than his wife wore; it had a grip on his mind, a grip on his finances and a grip on his God-given authority, all of which he'd relinquished just to appease the lusts of his flesh. She looks around, hoping to find a post, a video, a sermon or an article that will teach her how to deliver the man she'd sinned to get. She'd taken a shortcut to get him, but the road to deliverance and wholeness seems to be endless. Years later, she finds herself standing in front a lawyer. She'd married the fantasy of who she thought her husband was, but she was ready to divorce his reality. The minute she lifted her boundaries and her skirt, she'd given perversion a voice in her life, and anyone who has ever been romantically linked to a sexual deviant can tell you that they don't get fully delivered when they fall out at the altar. No! It's a lifelong battle that they have to fight. And every time she logs onto a computer that she shares with her husband, she knows that there is a high probability that she's going to get up disgusted or, at minimum, he will be constantly deleting the computer's history and cookies in an attempt to hide his search history. This is the penalty that she has elected to pay because she thought that she could take a shortcut through sin to get to her blessing. She thought that she could hijack her next season. And it's not just women who do this, of course! I've seen men marry women that they should have run from, only to have those women slowly turn them away from God. How so? Their wives would emotionally punish or physically neglect them whenever they didn't fit their wives' perspectives of what they each wanted in a husband. She wanted a carnal man with a hint of Christianity; she wanted a man who could pray down Heaven but give anyone that challenged them a slice of hell. She wanted mixture, and this is the evidence that she was a bondwoman or a bound woman. "Cast that bondwoman out!" Sarah yelled at Abraham after watching Ishmael mocking Isaac or, better yet, watching the counterfeit trying to silence the promise. This is because bound people bind people. The most commonly used binding agent that Satan uses are relational. In other words, he will use believers and unbelievers alike to carry out his agenda. As a matter of fact, the evidence that someone is bound is found in their fruit; the Bible tells us this. If a person doesn't respect the Word of God, but will, instead, repeatedly infringe upon the boundaries that God has created, that person is in bondage. What's his or her assignment? To bind and silence any and everyone who dares to say, "I love you," to him or her. The ties used to romantically bind someone are called soul ties. Another word for an ungodly soul tie is called a yoke. Soul ties are the zip ties of the spirit realm. They can't stop God's children from going to Heaven, but they can restrict their movements in the Earth realm, making them less effective.

In short, repentance is acknowledging the Word of God as truth, not just verbally, but through our choices. Oxford Languages defines the word "repent" this way: "feel or express sincere regret or remorse about one's wrongdoing or sin." The Greek word for "repent" is "metanoeó" and

Strong's Concordance defines it as "change my mind, change the inner man (particularly with reference to acceptance of the will of God), repent." What this means is that without embracing new information, it is nearly impossible to truly repent. Don't get me wrong, we can be sympathetic and even regretful of our sins, and many believers confuse these feelings with repentance, when they are not. They precede repentance but are not the actual event itself. Remember that the conscious mind is the waiting room of the soul. A man can have the Word of God and all of the wisdom his father taught him sitting in his conscious mind, but because he's never accepted or rejected this information, it has little to no weight in his life. Nevertheless, if that same man were to find himself in a hard situation, for example, he may start searching his heart for answers. There, he'd find all of the information he has never given weight to sitting in the waiting room of his heart, while all the lies he's come to believe are sitting in the subconscious or the center of his heart. In that moment, he may begin to reject the lies and embrace the truth. This is when you'll find him saying things like, "My Dad used to tell me all the time that love without God is nothing but vapor; it doesn't exist. But I didn't listen to him. And the scriptures say that God is love." Now, all of a sudden, he has exchanged the lies for the truth. In other words, he's repented. How so? He's taken the lies out of his subconscious and downgraded them back to his conscious mind. He then took the truth out of his conscious mind and placed it in his conscious. The truth will then set him free, meaning, it will create enough evidence to finally annihilate the lies that are lurking in his conscious. This is a form of deliverance. It's not necessarily casting the devil out, but it's casting the lies out so that they can be cast down. Nevertheless, if we don't repent, we have to endure the penalties of our choices. The penalty is not God's way of getting revenge. Penalties are designed to get us to redirect our steps. Let's look at another scripture.

1 Corinthians 5:1-5: It is actually reported that there is sexual immorality among you, and of a kind that is not tolerated even among pagans, for a man has his father's wife. And you are arrogant! Ought you not rather to mourn? Let him who has done this be removed from among you. For though absent in body, I am present in spirit; and as if present, I have already pronounced judgment on the one who did such a thing. When you are assembled in the name of the Lord Jesus and my spirit is present, with the power of our Lord Jesus, you are to deliver this man to Satan for the destruction of the flesh, so that his spirit may be saved in the day of the Lord.

Apostle Paul literally told the Corinthian Church to turn over those incestuous young men to Satan! If we prayed prayers like this nowadays, we'd definitely be accused of witchcraft! But why would the Apostle tell them to turn a person over to Satan? Isn't that cruel? Notice the intention behind it. He said that this was so that the young man's spirit could be saved. Again, penalties are designed to make us repent; they are not designed to torture and humiliate us, even though we may feel tortured and ashamed whenever we start reaping what we've sown.

Understanding Penalties

There's a penalty for crossing boundaries, and one of the greater penalties is death. If you cross over the North Korean border and attempt to enter South Korea, you'll either be arrested or shot. If you cross the Durand Line, the boundary that separates Afghanistan from Pakistan, you will be arrested or shot. If a prisoner tries to escape prison, he or she will be arrested or shot. There are penalties for crossing boundaries, and the most common of them is bondage. Consider the parable of the unforgiving servant.

Matthew 18:23-35: Therefore is the kingdom of heaven likened unto a certain king, which would take account of his servants. And when he had begun to reckon, one was brought unto him, which owed him ten thousand talents. But forasmuch as he had not to pay, his lord commanded him to be sold, and his wife, and children, and all that he had, and payment to be made. The servant therefore fell down, and worshipped him, saying, Lord, have patience with me, and I will pay thee all. Then the lord of that servant was moved with compassion, and loosed him, and forgave him the debt. But the same servant went out, and found one of his fellowservants, which owed him an hundred pence: and he laid hands on him, and took *him* by the throat, saying, Pay me that thou owest. And his fellowservant fell down at his feet, and besought him, saying, Have patience with me, and I will pay thee all. And he would not: but went and cast him into prison, till he should pay the debt. So when his fellowservants saw what was done, they were very sorry, and came and told unto their lord all that was done. Then his lord, after that he had called him, said unto him, O thou wicked servant, I forgave thee all that debt, because thou desiredst me: Shouldest not thou also have had compassion on thy fellowservant, even as I had pity on thee? And his lord was wroth, and delivered him to the tormentors, till he should pay all that was due unto him. So likewise shall my heavenly Father do also unto you, if ye from your hearts forgive not every one his brother their trespasses.

This scripture is symbolic, of course. The master is a type and shadow of Jesus Christ. The servant represents believers, and the fellow-servants are used to represent our brothers and sisters in Christ. Here, the unforgiving servant had been forgiven by his master, just as Jesus has taken on our sins for us. Nevertheless, when the time came for him to forgive one of his brothers or sisters in the Lord, he would not. What's worse is, his crimes or sins against God were far worse than whatever his fellow-servant had done to him. And yet, he refused to forgive the guy, but instead, chose to place him in bondage. When the master (Jesus Christ) heard of this, He summoned the man to Himself and questioned him about his behavior. He then withdrew his grace from the man (most Christians don't like this type of teaching), tossed him into prison (bondage) and into the hands of the tormentors (demons). The guy in question wasn't an unbeliever; he was a believer! What was his crime? He had not loved his brother enough to release him. Instead, he chose to bind someone after he himself had just finished begging for deliverance! This puts to bed (once and for all), this common belief that has slithered into the body of Christ—an assumption that believers can go into sin, hang out with the world and partake of their sins, all the while retaining their freedom in the name of evangelism. No! Bondage and freedom are two completely separate systems that are instituted in both kingdoms (the Kingdom of God and the kingdom of darkness), but they produce different results in both kingdoms. For example, as a servant of the Most High God, I am blessed, but in sin, I am not "above" the consequences. I often give this example so that people can understand the heart of God—if I had sex outside of marriage and I repented after the act was done, the consequences could and would still follow me. For example, if I discovered two months later that I was pregnant, does this mean that God hasn't forgiven me? No! But the system of the Kingdom is this—whatever a man sows, that shall he also reap! If I sow a seed, I will have to reap what comes behind it, even if what comes behind it weighs seven pounds and eleven ounces. If the man was "unclean," he would pass whatever issue he had to me. Would repentance set me free? Nope. I could possibly go through deliverance; God surely could heal me, but this process could potentially take years. Why? Because fornication is a baby crime! If I partook of this, it could only mean that I'm a babe in Christ or I'm intentionally, knowingly and rebelliously challenging the Word of God because I don't have enough faith to believe God for a husband. Or I could be mad at God for making me wait so long. Because of the long wait, I could have reasoned within myself that He needed my help, so I would have invested a sin offering into the relationship, hoping to speed things up and solidify the relationship. The point is you cannot (logically or spiritually) use bondage to free people!

Honestly, it would be interesting to write this chapter from a demon's perspective. How so? If I were a devil trying to oppress and bind God's people, I'd discuss the many recipes that I'd come to learn over the years for bondage. I'd point out the many people, both small and great, who've fallen into some of the tiniest of snares, and consequently, set their families up to be bound for generations on end. I'd end my convention by telling every disembodied devil how easy it is for them to find a person to possess today in a matter of minutes! If the person is Christian, I'd tell them how to find someone to oppress. I'd tell them:

- "There's power in their confessions!" I'd say. "Find a few musicians who's willing to do anything to get a big break and raise them up, but make sure you pervert them even more. This way, they'll sell perverted music and the people will sing the lyrics! When they do this, they are making confessions over themselves, and at the same time, they are slowly becoming desensitized to sin since the music will make it appear to be harmless fun! And get this—you'll be able to eventually bind them!

- "We need loud, immature, double-minded Christians on the forefront who are sick and tired of trying to live right! We need people who love their sins so much that they promote sin more than they promote the Word and will of God. We need to station them in the church and have them convicting Christians who are trying to lead godly lives. Have them call those folks religious. Here's the bonus—once you're able to find and bind them, they will then begin to speak against any and every Christian who dares to promote holiness! They'll gather together in numbers and call these types of people religious, thus, normalizing perversion, all the while, demonizing holiness!"

- "Find the Christians who are in idolatry and promise to give them whatever they want in exchange for sin. Pair them up with the double-minded Christians so they won't feel guilty whenever they sin. The double-minded will defend them if someone tries to rebuke them!"

- "Find the Christians who have yet to publish or publicly state their boundaries. Send a little romantic warfare their way, and let's see who takes the bait."

A month later, I would bring up the top binding demons to testify of how effective they were and how easy it was to bind Christians. I'd have them share what they'd learned with other demons, and we'd continue to escalate our assault against the faith. Some may argue that I'm giving the devil ideas; such a suggestion indicates that the person in question has been sleeping under a religious rock. Satan's been doing this mess for years! Understand that true warfare often involves spies; these are the people who sit in an organization or go into a place disguising themselves as allies, friends and lovers when, in truth, they are foes with friendly faces.

- "No man can serve two masters: for either he will hate the one, and love the other; or else he will hold to the one, and despise the other. Ye cannot serve God and mammon" (Matthew 6:24).
- "A double minded man is unstable in all his ways" (James 1:8).
- "For he that wavereth is like a wave of the sea driven with the wind and tossed. For let not that man think that he shall receive any thing of the Lord" (James 1:6).

Satan has been plotting and binding Christians and non-Christians for thousands of years, after all, there is nothing new underneath the sun or the Son. And for thousands of years, there have been believers who've been dancing between the world and the church. They come into the church smelling like the world, and they go into the world smelling like the church. What they're doing is called cross-pollinating. What is cross pollination? Science Direct explains it this way:

"Cross-pollination is the process of applying pollen from one flower to the pistils of another flower. Pollination occurs in

nature with the help of insects and wind. This process can also be done by hand to produce offspring with desired traits, such as color or pest resistance."
(Source: ScienceDirect/Methods of Cross Breeding/Pollen and Pollination/Laurent Crespel, Jacques Mouchotte)

Satan has wanted to cross-pollinate with the Kingdom of God ever since the day he laid eyes on Adam and Eve. This is why he convinced Eve to sin against God. He had his own kingdom, and he'd tempted her to submit herself under his rule. Of course, she didn't realize what she was doing, and she definitely didn't know his intentions. Nevertheless, she fell into the trap and Satan thought he'd created a hybrid—a cross between light and darkness; a bridge that would allow him to, once again, stand before God. After all, he hadn't planned to get kicked out of Heaven. He actually thought he'd win a war against the Most High God when, in truth, he wasn't (and still isn't) big enough to effectively come against Him. No one is. God didn't have to lift a finger because Satan was not and is not His equal, contrary to popular belief. Michael and his angels fought against Satan and his angels, and God's angels prevailed. And now, Satan is still trying to find a way to mix the church with the world. This is why we see people calling themselves Christian witches; this is why we see the LGBT community trying to change the Bible and the laws that were birthed because of it. In no other faiths do we see this behavior. You don't (and will probably never) see people calling themselves Muslim witches and you don't (and will probably never) see the

LGBT community going up against the Muslim faith about their beliefs. This is because Yahweh is the only God who can take Satan down! Again, Satan wants the ability to reign and be "like God" without the consequences that he knows he has to face at some point.

How interesting it is that in the natural, both insects and wind are used to cross-pollinate?! Biblically, insects were often used as plagues or punishment, and of course, we all should know Ephesians 4:14, which reads, "That we henceforth be no more children, tossed to and fro, and carried about with every wind of doctrine, by the sleight of men, and cunning craftiness, whereby they lie in wait to deceive." Insects, like demons, are the penalties that people pay for either having no boundaries, refusing to enforce their boundaries, having fluid boundaries or trespassing against any boundaries that have been put in place. This makes me think of my childhood, and how it had been plagued by roaches. I remember growing up with these nasty critters in our home. It didn't matter where we lived (we moved quite a bit), we almost always had roaches. Of course, this was because of a system that we had in our family. We had giant garbage cans that would sit in our house for days slowly filling up with food. And while we washed the dishes everyday, they would often sit in the sink for hours on end before we even thought to touch them. All the same, there were days when we managed to not wash the dishes, plus, my brother was known to hide food debris under his bed. Anytime there's a cleanliness issue in a home or building that is not immediately AND consistently addressed, a roach manifestation will be inevitable.

I don't have roaches now because, from the moment I rented my first home, I was passionately determined to not have to deal with those critters. What's funny is, the first house that I rented had a major roach infestation when I moved in. I remember sitting on the floor in the house my ex and I had just moved into. It was our first day there and I'd just returned from McDonald's. I sat on the floor to eat my food, only to have a few roaches come out and start making their way towards me. I was around 21-years old, but in that moment, I began to bawl like a child. I'd grown up with roaches and there was no way I was about to share another home with them. "I can't live with roaches!" I cried as I stood to my feet with my food in my hand. You see, I'd spent the last two years in a roach-free home, and the thought of having to deal with them again felt unbearable. Of course, we didn't know that the house had an infestation when we'd rented it. "I'm sorry! I can't live here! I can't live here!" It was almost as if I had PTSD. In that moment, I was genuinely ready to reject the house, even though we'd paid our first month's rent and deposit, plus, we'd signed a one-year lease. The few things that we had were already in the house, but I didn't care. My ex made a few phone calls, and I remember someone suggesting that we purchase some Bengal™ Roach Spray. It was guaranteed to kill all of the roaches in a home. We ended up getting six cans of Bengal™, a few tubes of Raid™ Roach Gel, and some boric acid. For the first day or two, we sprayed every corner and crevice with the spray. We put boric acid behind the fridge and the stove, and we placed the roach gel in the corners of the molding. By days two and three, our labor began to pay off. Every day, we would return to the house from our jobs and find roach carcasses everywhere. That house had a major infestation! We'd sweep them up and throw them out, and this continued for around a week. Before long, our house was completely roach-free. But here's the thing. Cleansing the house was one event; keeping it infestation free was another one. I'm not sure if the internet was a thing at that time (I don't remember it being so), but we didn't have a computer so we couldn't research ways to keep our newly cleansed house roach free. Nevertheless, we asked around and got the answers we needed. Here's what we learned:

1. Never leave food debris in the house overnight. If you have food trash, be sure to take it outside as soon as you can.

2. Buy small wastebaskets, not huge trashcans. Huge trashcans take days to fill up; this encourages you to leave food debris in the trashcan for days at a time.

3. Don't leave water in the sink. Roaches are called water-bugs for a reason; they can survive without food for one month but can only survive for one week without water. So, after washing your dishes, immediately dry out your sink.

4. Don't leave wet pet food out in the open overnight.

5. If your neighbors have a roach infestation (especially if you live in an apartment), you are likely to have one

as well. You'll have to be extra clean and spray or bomb your home every few months just to remain critter free. Also, encourage cleanliness with them by telling them some of the chemicals and processes you used to rid your home of roaches.

6. Be careful what you move into your home. If there are roaches in, for example, your furniture, they will move with you.

7. Roaches, like every other living thing, defecate. Even after you've killed them off, you need to purge your house of their residue (bodies and poop). If you do not, other roaches will smell the residue and invade your place.

Of course, there's a lesson behind these pointers; this isn't a "how to deliver your house from roaches" tutorial. The point is—roaches were the result of the previous tenants' choices. Every action provokes a reaction, and every reaction provokes another reaction. This story is never-ending; that is, unless someone interrupts it with a different choice—one that is both powerful and consistent. This almost reminds me of those psychic shows. I haven't seen any in years, but I remember watching an episode of one several years ago. On this episode, there were children who had been labeled as "gifted" because they knew things that other children didn't know. Normally when this happens, one of the parents or grandparents is said to have this gift, and of course, the world is fascinated with it. I remember one of the women saying that, because her daughter was so gifted, she would often get the attention of both good spirits and bad spirits. I was young in the faith when I watched this, but I knew that the spirits masquerading themselves as good spirits were actually evil spirits. The mother had moved her daughter around a lot because she was said to be sensitive to certain homes; she could feel the energy in the house and immediately know what had taken place in the residence. In other words, the mother blamed the demonic harassment her daughter had been enduring on the houses they lived in. But to her dismay, no matter how much they moved, her daughter continued to be spiritually harassed. I was screaming at the television, "That's because the demons are not in the houses; they're in you and your daughter, ma'am!" Of course, the mother couldn't hear me, so I settled with just hearing myself, wishing I had a few minutes alone with that mother to teach her what little I did know about the spirit world. Her daughter was infested with demonic spirits, and the mother had welcomed them in because they brought her daughter (and herself) both fame and money. Evil spirits are like roaches; they are nasty creatures who need to be addressed and removed.

Acts 16:16-21: And it came to pass, as we went to prayer, a certain damsel possessed with a spirit of divination met us, which brought her masters much gain by soothsaying: The same followed Paul and us, and cried, saying, These men are the servants of the most high God, which shew unto us the way of salvation. And this did she many days. But Paul, being grieved, turned and said to the spirit, I command thee in the name of Jesus Christ to come out of her. And he came out the same hour. And when her masters saw that the hope of their gains was gone, they caught Paul and Silas, and drew them into the marketplace unto the rulers, and brought them to the magistrates, saying, These men, being Jews, do exceedingly trouble our city, and teach customs, which are not lawful for us to receive, neither to observe, being Romans.

Sure, the children on the show were bound, but they were also being spiritually prostituted by their parents. Consider a story that CNN broken in 2013 regarding a Cambodian mother who'd sold her daughter into prostitution. Here's the story:

> "When a poor family in Cambodia fell afoul of loan sharks, the mother asked her youngest daughter to take a job. But not just any job. The girl, Kieu, was taken to a hospital and examined by a doctor, who issued her a 'certificate of virginity.' She was then delivered to a hotel, where a man raped her for two days. Kieu was 12 years old.
> 'I did not know what the job was,' says Kieu, now 14 and living in a safehouse. She says she returned home from the experience 'very heartbroken.' But her ordeal was not over. After the sale of her virginity, her mother had Kieu taken to a brothel where, she says, 'they held me like I was in prison.'
> She was kept there for three days, raped by three to six men a day. When she returned home, her mother

148

sent her away for stints in two other brothels, including one 400 kilometers away on the Thai border. When she learned her mother was planning to sell her again, this time for a six-month stretch, she realized she needed to flee her home.

'Selling my daughter was heartbreaking, but what can I say?' says Kieu's mother, Neoung, in an interview with a CNN crew that travelled to Phnom Penh to hear her story.

Like other local mothers CNN spoke to, she blames poverty for her decision to sell her daughter, saying a financial crisis drove her into the clutches of the traffickers who make their livelihoods preying on Cambodian children. 'It was because of the debt, that's why I had to sell her,' she says. 'I don't know what to do now, because we cannot move back to the past.'"

(Source: CNN/The Women Who Sold Their Daughters into Sex Slavery/by Phnom Penh, Cambodia)

What's the difference between the women who called their children gifted and rented them out to the media to have their "gifts" televised for the world to see versus Kieu's mother? There is none! The only credible argument they could have is that they didn't realize they were playing with demons, whereas the mothers who prostituted their daughters have some knowledge of the damage their daughters will endure both mentally and physically before they agreed to prostitute them. Nevertheless, they would argue that they didn't fully understand the spiritual implications or how their daughters would weather the trauma mentally. The point is, whenever boundaries are not put in place and enforced, either naturally or spiritually, filthy people and filthy spirits will move into the unguarded soul and start their reign. It's very similar to roaches and other pests that tend to move into homes. Again, roaches are like demons. Your house has boundaries (walls), but if you don't keep the house clean, you pretty much make those walls irrelevant. As it is in the natural, so it is in the spirit! You may have solid boundaries in place. For example, you may be abstaining from premarital sex, you may be surrounding yourself with good people and you may be fasting often. Howbeit, if you have unrepentant sin in your life, that sin will serve as demon food. In this case, demonic entities won't have to sit in the waiting room; instead, your rebellion gives them an all-access pass to your heart. All the same, deliverance is just one event in a lifelong process. Maintaining your freedom is the real challenge. How so? Because the enemy is going to use people to reject, abandon, neglect, persecute and oppress you. This is a human experience that we all endure! In other words, the enemy is going to try to get you to keep growing demonic fruit in your life; this way, he can stall God's system in your life by installing his own system; this allows him to begin his ascension into your soul. That is until you find yourself on the brink of insanity ready to jump into the bottomless pit of suicide. Unrepentant sin is the recipe for bondage! Being extremely carnal is the recipe for bondage, after all, demons love to feast on flesh that has not been crucified! This is because flesh bears ungodly fruit, and this fruit invigorates him!

Galatians 5:19-21: Now the works of the flesh are manifest, which are these; Adultery, fornication, uncleanness, lasciviousness, idolatry, witchcraft, hatred, variance, emulations, wrath, strife, seditions, heresies, envyings, murders, drunkenness, revellings, and such like: of the which I tell you before, as I have also told you in time past, that they which do such things shall not inherit the kingdom of God.

Matthew 7:16-20: Ye shall know them by their fruits. Do men gather grapes of thorns, or figs of thistles? Even so every good tree bringeth forth good fruit; but a corrupt tree bringeth forth evil fruit. A good tree cannot bring forth evil fruit, neither *can* a corrupt tree bring forth good fruit. Every tree that bringeth not forth good fruit is hewn down, and cast into the fire. Wherefore by their fruits ye shall know them.

What exactly is bondage? Dictionary.com defines it this way:
- slavery or involuntary servitude; serfdom.
- the state of being bound by or subjected to some external power or control.
- the state or practice of being physically restrained, as by being tied up, chained, or put in handcuffs, for sexual gratification.
- Early English Law. personal subjection to the control

of a superior; villeinage.

Bondage means to be a slave to something or someone. It means to be restricted, limited, restrained, constricted or walled in. And of course, there are many binding agents that Satan uses to bind people, many of which don't always involve the (continued) use of demons. They involved human will. You see, if there's anything that you want more than God, Satan has already gotten a grip on your heart and your future! All he has to do is hold your idol over your head, promising to give it to you if you'll enter an agreement with him. This is the very temptation he tried to plague Jesus with. Luke 4:5-8 details this temptation; it reads, "And the devil, taking him up into an high mountain, shewed unto him all the kingdoms of the world in a moment of time. And the devil said unto him, All this power will I give thee, and the glory of them: for that is delivered unto me; and to whomsoever I will I give it. If thou therefore wilt worship me, all shall be thine. And Jesus answered and said unto him, Get thee behind me, Satan: for it is written, Thou shalt worship the Lord thy God, and him only shalt thou serve." What's ironic is, Satan still uses this brand of temptation today. He understands the systems of the human mind, so he knows how to get you to bind yourself without the (continued) use of demons. He knows that if he causes someone close to you (parent, sibling, spouse) to hurt you repeatedly, he can write you off as broken. Broken people break people. They rebel against systems and authority, and they are always guarding themselves out of fear of being broken again. Consequently, they sabotage covenant relationships, they trust the wrong people and they chase platforms that they're not mature enough to mount. This is because they want to tell their stories, either directly or passively. They want to humiliate the people who once humiliated them. They want to hurt the people who once hurt them. They want to cause those people to feel intimidated by them, jealous of them and angry with them. And while the people in question are likely demonically bound, the use of demons is not necessary because of the systems in place in their lives. Satan believes God; the average believer doesn't! Satan understands the principles of sowing and reaping. The average believer has knowledge but little to no understanding of this concept. This is what it means to be deceived. Galatians 6:7 warns us this way, "Be not deceived; God is not mocked: for whatsoever a man soweth, that shall he also reap." What does it mean to reap? It means to gather the harvest. So, if you plant corn, be prepared to reap corn. If you plant corn, don't go out in the field looking for grapes. God is always using the natural realm in an attempt to help us understand the spirit realm. In the natural, for example, I wouldn't plant an apple tree and then act surprised whenever it produced apples. In the natural, I could own a plot of land, but I don't necessarily need wisdom to know that if I haven't planted a garden on that land, I'm not going to get a harvest. Howbeit, many of today's believers actually reason that they can reap a harvest that they have not sown, and they call it warfare whenever they reap the harvests that they have actually sown! If we behaved like this in regard to natural events, we'd be written off as crazy, however, we tend to turn a blind eye to believers who behave like this regarding spiritual things. Again, this is because we haven't fully studied the concept or the laws of sowing and reaping, therefore, we often sow into the kingdom of darkness, and then, we rush over to the Kingdom of God constantly looking for a harvest.

"I receive it!" The shouts coming from the crowd are almost deafening. Watching people leap from their seats to rejoice can be exhilarating; that is, until you realize that many of them have absolutely no seeds in the ground. Many of today's Christians won't serve anyone, won't sow any seeds, won't forsake their comfort zones and won't sacrifice anything. However, those same believers will shout the loudest in church and be some of the most animated people that you'll ever see, hoping that God will override His own system of sowing and reaping to bless and prosper them. This is because the spirit of poverty has deafened the ears of so many believers; the enemy has convinced many in the church that burning out all of their energy in a praise break is the shortcut to a blessing. You see, Satan doesn't mind us being religious; he just doesn't want us being faith-filled. Of course, praise breaks are awesome, but they were never designed to replace obedience; they cannot and do not replace the laws of sowing (works, choices) and reaping (rewards, penalties). What is sowing and what is reaping? Let's look at a few definitions.

Sow:

- to scatter (seed) over land, earth, etc., for growth; plant (Dictionary.com).
- to plant seed for growth especially by scattering (Merriam Webster).
- to set something in motion: begin an enterprise (Merriam Webster).

Reap:
- to gather by reaping: harvest (Merriam Webster).
- to cut (wheat, rye, etc.) with a sickle or other implement or a machine, as in harvest (Dictionary.com).
- to obtain or receive something as a result of your own actions (Collins Dictionary).

To sow simply means to plant; the secular word for "sow" is "invest." There is a difference between sowing and spending. Sowing typically involves faith and strategy, for example, a farmer has to know the best procedures, the best fertilizers and the best seasons to plant his or her harvest in. This is called knowledge. He then goes out and waters the land, even though no one, including himself, can see anything budding from it; this is called faith. He continues to do this day after day. All the same, he occasionally turns the ground and fights away any pests that would try to consume his harvest; this is called understanding. Once the bud breaks the ground, the farmer has to continue caring for the plant until it reaches full harvest; this is called revelation. To reap, on the other hand, simply means to harvest whatever it was that you've sown. Whatever you reap will either be a reward or a penalty; it will either be a surplus in your life or a deficit. And of course, you have to know when to reap. The Spruce(website) gives the following information regarding harvesting corn:

> "When you look at an ear of corn in the garden, you will see tassels at the end of the ear. These tassels, which include the cornsilk, are the part of the plant that both bears and receives the pollen. When corn is ready to harvest, the cornsilk turns from a light blond color to a dark brown. When the cornsilk is dark brown all the way down to the husk, you can assume that the corn is ready to eat" (Source: The Spruce/How and When to Pick and Cook Sweet Corn/Lauren Arcuri).

The system of sowing and reaping can be summed up in two words: action and reaction. Whatever you say and do can and will be held against you or for you. Every time you make a choice and you invest energy, time and effort into that choice, you provoke a response from either the natural or spiritual realm. Take a moment right now and clap your hands three times. Do you hear the sounds that were emitted? That's your response. You put your hands together and a sound was produced. If there are people with or around you, they will likely hear the sound of you clapping your hands, and this will provoke them to speak. Once they speak, they will expect you to respond again, but this time, verbally. This is because every action (seed) produces a reaction (harvest); every conversation is ongoing until it is silenced by the truth. There are conversations that were initiated thousands of years ago that are still going on today. The people who started those conversations are no longer in the land of the living, however, archaeologists, historians, scientists, theologians and teachers are still participating in those conversations to this very day, and they still haven't settled the many debates that started before Christ wrapped Himself in flesh and came into the Earth realm. All the same, there are conversations that your ancestors started that are still going on in your family today. We call them generational wealth or generational curses. Finally, there are conversations that you are starting or have started that will continue hundreds of years after you pass away. Words are said to lose their sound once they're spoken, but they don't lose their momentum. You are still living under the prayers and intercessions of family members who died hundreds of years before you entered the Earth. The point is, whatever you do continues with or without you. Whatever you say continues with or without you. Whatever you sow, you will reap, and whatever you reap, you will ultimately sow again. To break this vicious cycle, you have to uproot everything that violates God's ordinances and plant the right seeds. Please note that doing the wrong things for the right season is still not a good seed. This is called justification. Notice the word "justice" is the prefix of "justification." It also comes from the word "just" which means upright. Please understand that sin cannot stand before God. In other words, you can't take something that is crooked (perverted) and justify it. If and when we truly understand this, we'll wholeheartedly repent and start reaping the blessings of God. We'll stop trying to take shortcuts, only to find ourselves confronted by alligators (narcissists); we will no longer find ourselves running and falling face-forward into the many pits that Satan has dug in his kingdom. In the long-run, we all come to discover that God's way, albeit long, is the only way to a blessing.

Taking Back Control Over Your Life

Responsibility is the key to getting rid of the narcissist; this is how you kick the devil out of the driver's seat of your life. Please note that this isn't to discount your experience with the narcissist, but it is to help you to understand that the narcissistic/Jezebellic personality is a fine or a penalty we pay whenever we put someone before God and/or whenever we don't follow the ordinances of God. Sure, the narcissist may have lied to gain access to your life, and at that time, you hadn't done anything to invite this personality into your life. But that's called an attack. The narcissist is an opportunist, but keep in mind that an opportunist needs an opportunity. Whenever you extended that opportunity to the person, chances are, you hadn't followed through with the instructions outlined for believers in 1 John 4:1, which reads, "Beloved, do not believe every spirit, but test the spirits to see whether they are from God, for many false prophets have gone out into the world." But that's okay! We all fail, right? We all fall short of the glory of God! Nevertheless, the minute the narcissist began to show you his or her fruit, the ball rolled into your court; it was your time to respond. Remember, every action provokes a reaction, and every reaction provokes another action. When your turn came to respond, you still had the opportunity to walk away, but by this time, you didn't want to walk away. Maybe you were pregnant or you had a child with the narcissist. Maybe you had already exchanged vows with the narcissistic personality. Either way, the ball continually rolled into your court, but like most of us, you swatted it away. Again, this is not good, but it's what we do; we're humans! Howbeit, there's a lesson in all things. Let's go back to the story we read earlier. The young man took the route his mother told him not to take and consequently, he ended up enduring everything from insect bites, destroying his shoes, falling face-forward in the mud, and being confronted by an alligator. He'd disobeyed his mother, and because of this, he arrived at his trip had been severely delayed. The point is—you have to know how powerful, anointed and loved you are; this way, you won't entertain wild people. Sure, they have potential; everyone does! Even the heroin addict who slurs his speech has potential! Potential is a bunch of unfertilized eggs resting in the waiting room of our souls. Please read this carefully—whenever those eggs are fertilized by mere humans, they produce in and of themselves! So, if you cast your pearls (wisdom) to swine, what will be born to this union is called frustration, depression, anxiety and wasted time. However, when those eggs are fertilized by the Word of God (not you throwing scriptures at the person or dragging him or her to church), the individual will experience what we refer to as rebirth or being born again. Remember, you can't save someone who doesn't want to be saved; you can't talk, sex or manipulate a demon out of being a demon. But whenever you consistently try to do just this, you will find yourself committing many spiritual laws, all of which come with penalties. Look at it this way—your heart is a vehicle that's supposed to be heading in a certain direction. If you stop off in the wrong regions of thought or if you start heading in the wrong direction, even for a brief stint, the narcissist or another toxic personality type will convince you to ride shotgun in this event that we call your life. In other words, that person will get in the drivers' seat of your life and drive you completely insane! This is the equivalent of allowing a demon to drive your care. I often tell people this—deliverance casts the devil from behind the wheel, but it does not turn the car around! Repentance does! But what repentance doesn't do is clean up the pain that we've endured when we were heading in the wrong direction. The pain is called residue. This is cleaned up whenever we forcefully turn our lives around and consistently chase the heart of God. In this, He heals our wounds and explains to us why we've suffered through whatever it is that we've suffered through.

Lastly, what if the narcissist is a parent? Is it still considered a penalty every time that parent hurts you? Not when you're a child, but whenever you become an adult, you are responsible for what happens to the adult-sized you. In 1

Corinthians 13:11, Apostle Paul said, "When I was a child, I spake as a child, I understood as a child, I thought as a child: but when I became a man, I put away childish things." As believers, we have often interpreted Paul's words to mean that he stopped behaving immaturely; he stopped playing games and started behaving as a man, and this interpretation is correct, but it's not complete. Consider this—narcissists and most toxic people are childish. All the same, the words "put away" also means to divorce. So, what Apostle Paul was also saying is—he divorced the mentality that attracted emotionally, mentally and spiritually unhealthy people in his life! He stopped being the victim and he decided to be the victor. Excuses and blame are childish things! When Adam sinned against God, he blamed Eve. When Eve sinned against God, she blamed the devil. Satan had no one to blame and no reason to blame anyone else because he was already condemned by then! There was no reason for him to deflect! What I'm saying here is, you have to stop dreaming of having a Brady Bunch type experience with your parents and just accept them for not just who they are, but how they are. But wait—this does NOT mean that you have to tolerate their toxic ways! It simply means that you have to finally be honest with yourself about them, and stop looking for the right words to change their minds! In short, share the gospel with your parents; this is called evangelism. Yes, even if they claim to already be saved (you will know them by their fruits). If the parent doesn't want the truth or only pretends to want the truth in order to get your hopes up again, you have to "put away" the childish thing. In other words, you have to divorce the belief that you will eventually find the password to free your parents so that you can all live happily ever after. You have to accept that one or both of your parents may remain toxic all the way up until his or her last day on Earth. When you accept and acknowledge this, it will provoke you to finally establish boundaries with that parent. You'll divorce the relationship you have with that particular parent (or parents) and establish one that is replete with boundaries and penalties, and these boundaries and penalties won't just be for the parental figure or figures. They'll also be for you because you'll see the importance in disciplining yourself. For example, if you have a parent who is abusive and condescending, you'll draw up some guidelines that this parent has to abide by in order to have access to you. This is NOT designed to punish or train the parent! This is for your mental health! You could start off by assessing how often you speak with that parent. You may have to drastically lessen the amount of times you speak and the length of each conversation. This means that you have to now start paying attention to yourself and your parent(s). Whenever you speak on the phone with that parent, how long does it take before he or she says something toxic? What are the signs that the parent is about to explode or say something abusive? You need to know this! What are your parents' triggers? What are your triggers? If your mother is always berating you for being single, don't discuss your relationship status or your former relationships with her. Don't tell her about any man or woman who is expressing interest in you. One part of putting away childish things is not having adult conversations with someone who is immature or in some cases, developmentally delayed because of trauma. Whenever your mother brings up the fact that you are single, it's time to get off the phone or leave her home. If she's at your house, it's time to send her home or, at minimum, you may need to go for a walk. But before you do any of this, you have to have a discussion with her, bringing to her attention the topics that typically trigger an emotional response from her. Tell her that you will no longer discuss these things with her, and if she brings them up and tries to start a fight, you will remove yourself from the discussion. And understand this—you may have to visit and see less and less of her; you have to study to see how much of you she can handle. See her as a child and yourself as an adult; don't look at her natural age, look at her emotional stage. You may have to go from speaking with her everyday to speaking with her once or twice a week for 15 minute intervals. Then again, if she's super toxic, you may have to speak to her once a month for ten minute intervals. If she's destroying you inside, you may have to speak with her once every six months to a year. Some people would encourage you to steer close to your mother, often reminding you that you have one mother and that you'll regret not being a present force in her life whenever she passes away. But in my experience, the people who regret the most are the ones who kept walking ear-to-ear with their toxic parents. This is because they were always at odds with one another, so much so that they either felt somewhat responsible for their parents' demise or they felt slighted because they never got a chance to see their parents mature and become the emotionally mature and stable people that they needed them to be. Consequently, they grew bitter towards their deceased parents. On the other hand, people who put the necessary amounts of space and time between themselves and their toxic parents, were able to heal and look at their parents' demise from a healthy perspective. They knew that they were not to blame for their parents' deaths. Many of them were able to maintain a healthy relationship with their toxic parents by speaking with them weekly or monthly. Because their mothers, for example, didn't have the space and the time to be incredibly toxic, she used her time with her relatively estranged children to discuss other things. And get this, if and whenever she started taking the conversation in a toxic direction, the people in question politely and respectively said, "Hey Mom, I'll call you back. Okay?" And they did just that; they called her later that day or later that week. The point is, they learned how to have a healthy relationship with a toxic person. Howbeit, if you try to force a toxic parent into a mold, you will not only further traumatize an already traumatized soul, but you may do irreparable damage to your relationship with that parent. If, on the other hand, you accept that your parent is broken and that you don't have the tools to fix that parent, you'll focus on building a loving relationship with the parent, even if this means that the two of you don't speak as often as you both want. And it goes without saying that you should offer counseling to the parent. Don't make your parents feel like they're crazy; don't make them feel like damaged goods. Just introduce therapy as an option to fix your relationship with your parent. If you can, pay for some one-on-one sessions with your parent(s) and a therapist. Make sure to get some counseling yourself as well! If you ask someone to go through therapy to fix your relationship with the person, but you refuse to go to therapy, this is the same as you saying to the individual that he or she is wrong and you're right. The point is—building a healthy relationship with a toxic parent is (in many cases) doable, but you have to study the science and the signs behind your relationship with the person and respond accordingly.

Remember, every opportunist needs an opportunity, and if you constantly give the opportunist what he or she needs to hurt and further damage you, you can no longer blame the narcissist or the toxic person for the condition of a heart that God told you to guard. You may be an empath (prophetic person), and if this is the case, understand that you are carrying something valuable; you are carrying with you an assignment from Heaven. When you don't know who you are, please note that Satan knows who you are and some of what you carry. How so? It's in your bloodline. If your parents are toxic, this is why they're in the condition that they're in! They never woke up to realize who they are; consequently, Satan attacked them without mercy. He built a siege wall around their souls and kept knowledge, wisdom, understanding, revelation and discernment out of their subconscious minds, all the while, allowing suspicion, rejection, fear of rejection and every other demonic principle and spirit into their subconscious minds. Simply put, they may have been prophetic souls with no covering! Prophetic people who don't truly know God and have no healthy relationships to draw from oftentimes become incredibly unstable and toxic. Consider the story of Elijah. He'd just come back from one of his greatest victories; he'd turned the heart of Israel back to Yahweh and he'd had them to slaughter the prophets of Baal, but then, he received a threat from Jezebel. Let's look at the story.

1 Kings 19:1-8 (ESV): Ahab told Jezebel all that Elijah had done, and how he had killed all the prophets with the sword. Then Jezebel sent a messenger to Elijah, saying, "So may the gods do to me and more also, if I do not make your life as the life of one of them by this time tomorrow." Then he was afraid, and he arose and ran for his life and came to Beersheba, which belongs to Judah, and left his servant there. But he himself went a day's journey into the wilderness and came and sat down under a broom tree. And he asked that he might die, saying, "It is enough; now, O Lord, take away my life, for I am no better than my fathers." And he lay down and slept under a broom tree. And behold, an angel touched him and said to him, "Arise and eat." And he looked, and behold, there was at his head a cake baked on hot stones and a jar of water. And he ate and drank and lay down again. And the angel of the Lord came again a second time and touched him and said, "Arise and eat, for the journey is too great for you." And he arose and ate and drank, and went in the strength of that food forty days and forty nights to Horeb, the mount of God.

Elijah was a prophet of the Lord, and like many empathic people, he was being pursued by a bloodthirsty narcissist who would stop at nothing to wipe him off the face of this planet. Because of this, Elijah's mental health began to deteriorate causing him to become suicidal. He'd done right by putting space between himself and the wicked Jezebel, but he'd done wrong by running from his assignment and allowing fear to drive him into isolation. Afterwards, he had an angelic encounter. The angel gave him food to eat, and after this, he fasted for forty days and forty nights. How often do you fast? Again, your parents may not have known who they are or were (most prophetic people never come to know their identities because they spend the entirety of their lives entertaining narcissists). However, you now know a part of who you are! You may not necessarily be a prophet, but if you are empathic, you are wired to be prophetic. This is why you're super sensitive; this is why you've dreamed about events and then saw those same events come to pass! Now that you know this, you have to take responsibility for your own life and you have to do the hard work of guarding your heart.

EMPATHS AND GIVING

One of the general complaints of givers and empaths is that they are often taken advantage of, especially by the covert and the overt narcissist. I've read articles and watched videos about empathy, because that's a secular term that readily describes one of my strengths in the natural. Empathy is characterized as a weakness, especially by dominant personality types, but this isn't true. Empathy is a God-given gift. Empaths are natural givers. As we discussed in Book One, many of us have what the Bible describes as the "gift of charity." 1 Corinthians 13:4-8 details this gift. It reads, "Charity suffereth long, and is kind; charity envieth not; charity vaunteth not itself, is not puffed up, Doth not behave itself unseemly, seeketh not her own, is not easily provoked, thinketh no evil; Rejoiceth not in iniquity, but rejoiceth in the truth; Beareth all things, believeth all things, hopeth all things, endureth all things. Charity never faileth: but whether there be prophecies, they shall fail; whether there be tongues, they shall cease; whether there be knowledge, it shall vanish away."

In other translations of the Bible, the word "charity" isn't used; instead, the word "love" is used to replace it. And this is accurate, to be honest because charity is an expression of love. Charity means to give generously from the heart. My mother had this gift and it was a major gift in her life, however, when the gift of charity is not guarded by discernment, wisdom and boundaries, the person who has it can (and often will) repeatedly put himself or herself in harm's way. This is because we live in a world full of takers; takers are consumers. They can be very unapologetic, self-centered and unsympathetic. And one of the most dangerous takers out there is the one who has unmet needs. The more unmet needs that a taker has, the more desperate and manipulative the taker will become. For example, have you ever come across someone who is always begging for money, always complaining about their situation and always trying to manipulate someone? These people are not always narcissistic, but they are very similar in many ways. One of the ways to differentiate the two is to look at their track records in your life. Narcissists don't mind giving if they believe that they'll get more in return. Takers, on the other hand, will give sparingly, but they often find ways to avoid giving, for example, using the term, "my situation." You may hear a woman saying, for example, "Yes, she let me move in with her, but she knew *my situation* before I moved in. That's why I don't understand why she's harassing me about rent. What little money that I do make, I had to pay a few of my bills with and get my hair done. I wasn't about to give her my last few dollars!" Now, this woman sounds narcissistic, but she may just be a taker. Takers can be and often are narcissistic or they have traces of narcissism in them, but for the most part, narcissism involves more traits. Howbeit, most empaths are givers. All the same, most empaths are prophetic. This doesn't mean that they're prophets; it simply means that God gave them a level of sensitivity that most people don't have. This is why empaths forgive easily and they give often. These traits often cause empaths to hate themselves or to hate their gifts, especially when those gifts are constantly being hijacked or, better yet, those gifts are always attracting narcissists and takers into their lives. But the gift isn't the problem; the giver is. You see, every gift has to be guarded because it's not only valuable, it's a weapon that God gave you to destroy the works of the enemy. Nevertheless, when you don't guard your gift (most of us have never been taught how to do this), you essentially become a gift with no bodyguard. This is like hiring a sweet old lady to drive an armored truck with no guards or guns to protect her. If the news got out that the driver of the armored truck was a helpless 88-year old woman, it wouldn't be long before her family would find themselves planning her funeral.

Empaths are energized whenever we give, but once this system is hijacked by the narcissist, it causes the empath to feel drained and taken advantage of. This works against the empath's self-esteem, causing the empath to withdraw himself or herself from people. Today, there are many empaths in isolation because they are afraid of takers and narcissists. Now, the word "narcissist" is the secular term for the Jezebel spirit, but the term "empath" has two faces:

1. **The Ahab:** In Satan's world, the empath is the infamous Ahab spirit. If you have allowed fear, procrastination and insecurity to drive you away from your God-given authority, your gift has been hijacked

by the enemy. This would mean that you need to educate yourself about the Ahab spirit and get delivered from it expeditiously!

2. **The Sower:** In God's Kingdom, the empath is the prophet or prophetic person; it is the giver! What did God say about givers? The Bible says that God gives seed to the sower. The word "sower" is just another term for giver.

Of course, not all givers are empaths, and not all empaths are prophets. Some are just prophetic, meaning, they have a level of sensitivity that allows them to sense God's presence, the presence of angels and the presence of demons. You may simply give because God impressed it upon your heart to do so. Nevertheless, it is important to know that the Jezebel spirit specifically targets prophets and prophetic types; one of its goals is to get you to despise your gift; this is to cause you to be afraid and suspicious of most people, worrying that they will take advantage of you, after all, that's what you've experienced for a large part of your life. I inherited the gift of charity from my mother and I despised the gift at first. To be honest, I was afraid of it. I'd seen her getting taken advantage of so much that I wanted to hide myself from the human race, only allowing one or two people into my world at a time. To be honest, I was terrified of the gift. I felt like if I walked in it, I was going to look up one day and find myself surrounded by folks who didn't love me, after all, that's what I saw happen to my mother. She died from a lack of boundaries; the doctors called it lung cancer, I call it as I witnessed it. But one day, the Lord began to deliver me from my fear of giving. You see, a giver never stops giving, but when the gift is perverted, it starts flowing in reverse. When my gift was perverted, I started hoarding. Now, don't get me wrong, my house has never been overrun by stuff. My house is very organized, spacious, and clean, however, hoarding doesn't always look like what we've seen on television (those people are extreme hoarders). Sometimes, hoarders become massive collectors of certain things, which is what I started doing. I started collecting perfumes, body sprays, shoes, and purses. And while these items never took over my home because I'm organized, I did have to invest in ways to keep them organized. I purchased hanging organizers and shelves. Before long, I realized that something was wrong because I wasn't using most of the perfumes. I just bought and stored them. To remedy this, whenever I had a visitor, I started taking them up to the room where I kept my perfume and giving them a few bottles of the perfumes or body sprays to take home with them. If they wore a size six in shoes, I'd overload them with brand new shoes that I'd never worn. My gift wanted to express itself, but I'd once tried to hide and constrict it. It didn't work. But the Lord ministered to me and I realized that my gift was never in trouble. You see, as beautiful as my mother was, I'm not my mother. I have always stood guard around everything that God has given me. Have I been taken advantage of? Yes, but no more than most people! So, my fears, while understandable, were unfounded.

Givers have an assignment from Heaven. Most givers were born to build and finance the Kingdom of God. They have a specific assignment to be conduits between Heaven and Earth, but when a prophetic person doesn't know who he or she is, that person will open his or her life (and heart) to broken, toxic and narcissistic souls. The narcissist's assignment is to unplug the giver. Again, this causes the gift of giving to go in reverse. Consequently, the empath begins to hoard anything he or she considers valuable, including his or her thoughts. You see, people who have this gift have been muzzled and silenced for so long that they often keep how they feel to themselves. Whenever they witness people hurting other people, they reason within themselves that it's not their business. This is why we have a society filled with people who will videotape a crime in progress, instead of helping the victim. Understand this—most givers are builders. Yes, even if they haven't built anything yet! They were designed to create; another word for a builder is a creative. Their wealth is supposed to be the conduits by which Heaven channels wealth to them, and they are supposed to be conduits by which God channels wealth to the Church at large. Satan knows this about them, but most of them don't know this about themselves! Because of this, many churches shut their doors for lack of funds. A better way to say this is—many churches shut their doors because they lack creatives! The prophets and prophetic types are oftentimes somewhere hiding in caves, being entertained by the very thing they should be avoiding—the narcissist! They are somewhere being traumatized, broken and perverted, so whenever they do come into the church, their gifts have gone in reverse. So, instead of giving to the church, they take from the church. If ever and whenever the church puts a limit on their resources, they become angry and withdraw themselves to their caves. And get this—their caves aren't always their homes! Sometimes, a perverted prophet or prophetic individual will withdraw himself or herself into religion; this is a common hiding place for creatives! And religion further silences them, binding them with the cords of guilt, shame, fear and hopelessness. Another common hiding place for empaths are relationships, whether those relationships are romantic, platonic or familial. For example, most empaths would rather be taken advantage of by a love interest than to feel taken advantage of by the church. So, they give their best years and resources to people. After this, they drag their bruised bodies and egos into the church, where they spend the next few years taking from the institution that they were designed to fund.

The word "empathic" is defined by Oxford Languages as "showing an ability to understand and share the feelings of another." It's the very same definition that they give for the word "empathetic." It represents a person's ability to relate to someone else. So, when we use the word "empathic," what we are really saying is an empathetic person. This is important because many occultic movements are using terms like "empath" to describe spiritually sensitive people who have supernatural abilities. This is great, but here's the issue—anytime you deal with the spirit realm, all the while, keeping the Holy Spirit out of your conversations, you are teaching people to practice witchcraft. And this is not surprising, given the fact that these occultic movements are driven by witches and witchcraft. Any attempt to access the spirit realm without the Spirit of God is dangerous! And people who do this oftentimes knowingly or unknowingly open their hearts to unclean spirits; these spirits then hijack their gifts, so whereas they were supposed to be prophetic, they become demonic. They become false prophets, and get this—not every false prophet sits in a church or has a ministerial title. Many of them simply call themselves psychics, witches, warlocks or whatever titles they choose to operate under. Consequently, they have gifted children who are also able to see into the realm of the spirit—children who either continue their legacy of witchcraft or they end up serving as demonic offerings. Get this—whenever you see a lot of premature death, sexual perversion, crime and mental illness in a family, you can almost always trace the issue back to someone in their ancestry pool who made a deal with the devil! In many cases, it was a great-great grandmother who was afraid of losing her philandering husband. This was common for many of our ancestors, especially those of us who are African American. Let me explain. We all know the history of African Americans in the United States. Our ancestors were brought here as slaves. In 1865, slavery was abolished, but this didn't mean that Blacks were free. They had to deal with another type of slavery called oppression and extreme racism. Segregation was the theme of that day, and in the South, Blacks were often beat, lynched and harassed, not only by civilians, but by law enforcement officers. Because of this, most African Americans did not trust the police. Their resources were extremely limited and information was withheld from the Black community.

During this time, divorce was unheard of! The same is almost true for birth control. So, whenever a woman got married, she was expected to make her traumatized husband happy. As a Black man, he'd been traumatized at school, at the store and just about everywhere he went. All the same, he was likely uneducated. This toxic duo made him a horrible husband. The women were traumatized as well, but segregationists didn't focus as much on women as they did men. Now, don't get me wrong, they raped and beat women, but they were determined to kill off Black men or, at minimum, bring them back under their oppressive thumbs. This is why I often encourage people to forgive their parents and grandparents; many of them raised our parents and many of them raised us while dealing with PTSD (Post Traumatic Stress Syndrome) and little to no education. But let's go back to the story. It was common for our great-great-great grandmothers to find themselves married to men who cheated on them and abused them. They couldn't call the cops out of fear of their husbands being brutally beaten or worse, killed. They couldn't escape to their parents' houses because they were oftentimes blamed for the conditions of their marriages. Their husbands (our great-great-great grandfathers) would have affairs with some of the women in their communities. Let's create a character; we'll call her Daphne. Let's say that Daphne was a young woman in the 1930's South. She ended up marrying a man named Darnell. Note: Daphne and Darnell are a type and shadow of many of our great-great-great grandparents. Darnell won over Daphne's father and got his permission to marry Daphne. During that time, there was no such thing as a birth control pill. Birth control consisted of condoms and sponges soaked in olive oil. And this costed money! Most African Americans were barely getting by. They simply could not afford birth control, and many of our ancestors simply did not believe in birth control. They believed that it was satanic, so they refrained from it, often opting to use the withdrawal method in their attempts to prevent pregnancy. Consequently, most African families consisted of seven to ten children. With an increasing amount of mouths to feed, Mr. Darnell became increasingly fearful and unstable. He blamed his wife for his issues because, as he would put it, she kept getting "knocked up." In an attempt to escape his issue, Mr. Darnell started drinking what they called Moonshine. Wikipedia reports the following: "Moonshine was originally a slang term for high-proof distilled spirits that were and continue to be produced illicitly, without government authorization." In truth, a lot of Moonshine was produced in the Black community; it was the drug of that time. And Mr. Darnell was bound by it. And the more he was oppressed on his job, the more he drank. The more he drank, the more volatile he became. Before long, he was beating and cheating on his wife regularly. Mrs. Daphne would even toss herself into harm's

way in an attempt to protect her children from her husband ,
and whenever she tried to leave him, her family and friends
would send her back home. "Fix yourself up sometimes!"
This was just one of the many abusive terms that Mrs.
Daphne and many of our ancestors heard whenever they
cried out for help. Again, this was because of oppression and
a lack of education. Abused people abuse people; simply
put. All the same, oppressed people oppress people, just like
hurt people hurt people.

To make matters worse, women were enduring another type
of oppression. Women were paid four times less than men
and could only work as teachers, nurses and maids. Black
women were paid even less than that! They didn't make
enough money to take care of themselves alone, so they
definitely could not afford to feed their children without their
husbands. With nowhere left to turn and seven mouths to
feed, Mrs. Daphne went home to her husband and the
beatings continued. And if this wasn't bad enough, his
cheating ways escalated when he met a woman named Ms.
Lula Mae. Ms. Lula was known for messing with married
men; the women of that time referred to her as a "floozy." Mr.
Darnell became bewitched by Ms. Lula Mae's rebellious
ways and her experience in the bedroom. All the same,
women like her oftentimes had no children or they had one
child who would often be off somewhere living with his or her
grandmother, so Ms. Lula Mae's house became the perfect
escape for a cheating man who wanted to get away from the
sounds of his children and his wife. Mr. Darnell began to

reason within himself that Ms. Lula Mae's house was more peaceful and tolerable than his own. He could get drunk and she wouldn't "nag" him. He could lie down without hearing the sounds of children playing, crying or being reprimanded by their mother. So, he became increasingly abusive. With nowhere left to turn, Mrs. Daphne turned to a few of her friends and discussed her fears with them. She was on the verge of losing her husband, and she had seven children who would be left fatherless and hungry. All the same, she knew who her husband's main mistress was. He'd cheated before, but there was something about Mrs. Lula Mae that made him nearly forget about every other "floozy" he had been seeing. "She got roots on your husband! No man would act like that unless somebody's got roots on him!" Believe it or not, this was a common way of reasoning and it was what Mrs. Daphne heard a couple of her friends saying. "Go talk to Madam Giselle over on 9th street. She can break those roots off him. She did it for my Aunt Eula, and since then, my Uncle Earl hasn't cheated!" Desperate and fearful, Mrs. Daphne started working as a maid and hiding some of her money. She even hid some of the money she got from her husband. She'd go to the store, buy the food for the house and hide the rest of the money. When she had enough money to pay Madam Giselle (the witch around the corner), she paid her a visit and gave her the money to break the "roots" or spell off her husband. Unbeknownst to her, she was entering into a demonic contract—one that would span several generations. And it worked! One of three scenarios would take place:

1. Her husband would catch Mrs. Lula Mae with another man, end up beating her up, and consequently, Mrs. Lula Mae would have him arrested. This forced him to return home to his wife who would see his arrest as God answering her prayers and saving her family. So, she wouldn't say a word. Instead, she would bail her husband out of jail and watch as Moonshine destroyed what was left of him.

2. Mrs. Lula Mae would meet, marry and move in with someone else, leaving Mr. Darnell brokenhearted and angry.

3. Mr. Darnell would find himself somewhat incapacitated after having an accident on his job or after having a car accident. His wife would finally be able to prove herself by taking care of him, all the while, Ms. Lula Mae would be entertaining someone else's husband.

4. Mrs. Lula Mae would end up dying. She would oftentimes die at the hands of one of her lovers.

Ask your grandparents or someone who was living between 1920-1940; they'll tell you that this was a common occurrence! This is how many unclean spirits entered our bloodlines. And generation after generation, Satan has oppressed many people because of these demonic contracts; that is, until someone arises who has what we call the "breaker's anointing." The "breaker" is oftentimes a prophetic individual born into a demonically bound and oftentimes religious family who goes against the grain of religion to pursue a relationship with the Most High God. This person is oftentimes the empath, and for whatever reason, Satan saw signs of many empaths' anointing when they were children. So, he used their traumatized parents to traumatize them. Of all of their parents' children, they were the ones who suffered through the most rejection, the most abuse and the most trauma. Nevertheless, try as he may, Satan was unable to break many of them. This is because whenever he attempted to break the breaker, he unintentionally activated their anointing. Don't get me wrong—many prophetic people have fallen in the wilderness, including many of them who were specifically wired to be breakers. Again, they were intercepted, overwhelmed and consumed by the narcissist. And by consumed, I mean that their mental space, time and peace was completely stolen from them by their narcissistic lovers. This is why the Bible warns us to guard our hearts and not awaken love before its time. Prophetic people are givers; we've established this, but what we need to also understand is that prophetic people are oftentimes filled with love. Again, many translations of the Bible use the word "love" in place of "charity," and while this is not error, it doesn't help us to understand the nature and makeup of charity. In order for me to be a giver, I must first have something to give. God gives the empath an overwhelming amount of love and compassion to share with others. Because of this, empathic people are almost always looking for someone or something to love. When this gift is broken and perverted, it goes in reverse. Consequently, many empaths or prophetic people become lovers of self, proud, boastful and double-minded. Many even become schizophrenic or start dealing with other mental/demonic issues that oftentimes go unaddressed. This is the aftermath of trauma. And like Elijah, many prophetic people become suicidal simply because they don't understand how they are wired or why they're suffering through the constant attacks of the narcissist. Nevertheless, whenever a breaker finally walks into the right church and comes to know and understand who he or she is, that prophetic personality will go through bouts of deliverance and restoration; this allows his or her gift to be unclogged, thus stopping it from going in reverse. The breaker then learns how to set boundaries with his or her bound family; that is, until the season comes when he or she is able to gather many of his or her family members and begin to set them free. In many cases, this happens over the course of time, whereas, the breaker doesn't always cast demons out of his or her family, but instead, leads them to understand why they behave and think the way they do. This provokes many of them to start their own exoduses out of religion and into relationship with God. And they get most, if not all, of their deliverance while walking out their newfound faith. But the empath has to take his or her own journey first. This is important because many empaths spend years arguing with and trying to force the eyes of their broken family members open. This is a waste of time and it can also be counterproductive. Matthew 7:5 instructs us this way, "Thou hypocrite, first cast out the beam out of thine own eye; and then shalt thou see clearly to cast out the mote out of thy brother's eye." In short, we have to go on our own exoduses first and get the freedom we need to free someone else. This journey could take years to complete, but it's well worth it! But in the meantime, it is important for the prophetic personalities to guard their gifts and their hearts. How is this done? As a giver or an empath, how do you keep yourself from being taken advantage of by predatory people? "But let your communication be, Yea, yea; Nay, nay: for whatsoever is more than these cometh of evil" (Matthew 5:37). Yes, it's that simple. Howbeit, below are a few tips that will surely help you to guard your gift.

1. Acknowledge that you are a giver. God gives seed to the sower. (Please note that God requires all believers to give, but there are some who are wired to be natural and supernatural givers. Again, these are the ones designed to be millionaires or multimillionaires; this is because God wants to raise them up to fund His Kingdom in the Earth.)

2. Establish sound barriers and boundaries around every area of your life. Remember, this is called zoning. Write a list of every area that needs to be guarded, and then, list as many rules, guidelines, restrictions and allowances around them as possible. Make sure that your list is reasonable, otherwise, you may end up creating inverted boundaries and imprisoning yourself.

3. Get in a good church and submit your gifts there. I can't stress this enough! Your gift is designed to be used by God for His benefit and the benefit of His Kingdom! Remember, we talked about the gears of a

system. The Kingdom's gears move clockwise and so should your gift. When you plug your gift into the Kingdom, for example, through your church, you won't have time to allow others to take advantage of them. At the same time, you'll come to value your gifts enough to not allow anyone to prostitute them or take advantage of them.

4. When you realize that you have been feeding or supplying a taker or a narcissist, don't panic; it's happened to the best of us! Just stop giving to that person. Utilize the power of no! No is a legal term that says to the taker, "You cannot trespass beyond this point." It also provokes you to say, "I will not go beyond that point."

5. Trust your discernment! Sowers are normally very discerning people; we have to be! And sometimes, our discernment is so keen and so sensitive that we question it, especially when we see everyone around us embracing folks that our discernment tells us to stay away from. This is what has gotten us in trouble many times before! We trusted everybody's judgment but our own and ended up having to pray a bunch of narcissists out of our lives because of this. No! If something feels odd or off about a person, pray about it and keep your distance from that person unless or until God says otherwise!

6. Start making people sign contracts! If a narcissist or a taker asks, for example, for money and promises to pay that money back, hand him or her a very detailed

contract and have that person to sign it. Make sure there's a witness available as well. Chances are, the narcissist or the taker will sign the contract and you'll have to take them to court or they will promise to sign the contract after "looking it over with their attorney" (this will never happen), and they'll never contact you again.

7. Stop telling people what you have! I know that sometimes, we get excited and want people to know what God has done, will do or is doing for us, but this isn't always a wise move. I had to learn to "shut up" and let God bless me, only stopping to testify later on down the road.

8. Let your yes be yes and your no be no. Don't add anything to it. If you say "no" to a person, don't give an excuse behind it. That's one of the biggest mistakes you can make. Again, I've witnessed firsthand how predators deal with the word "no." Normally, if you say, for example, "No, because I have to pay my rent," they'll come up with another question. "How much is your rent and when is it due? I'll pay you back before then." Or if you say, "I can't help you because I haven't been feeling my best lately," they'll typically respond, "What's wrong? Do you think you can help me next week then?" The best and least contested answer is a simple no, and if they question why, simply say, I have my own responsibilities to handle. Don't go any further than that.

9. Be willing to let the predatory person and/or people

exit your life. Predators like prey, and if you refuse to allow yourself to be preyed on, most predatory people will distance themselves from you.

10. Pacify your need to give by giving to your church and to the homeless. Get out and be a blessing to someone in need—someone who doesn't necessarily know your name or your phone number.

The Reemergence of Witchcraft

I was watching a Nigerian skit one day that pretty much summarized how witchcraft works. In the skit, a Nigerian guy happened to stroll by a structure, and he noticed a sign on the outside of that structure that read, "Eat anything you like. Your grandson will pay. Since 1972." At first, I was going to scroll right past the video, but those words caught my attention because it represented what I have been teaching for a long time. In the skit, the young man who happened to be strolling by was penniless, so when he saw the sign, he gasped in dismay. Curious and hungry, he wandered into the restaurant where he found a man washing dishes. He then questioned the man about the sign, and of course, the man confirmed that it was true. He could eat anything he wanted with no upfront costs to himself, and his future grandson would pay later. The sojourner could not believe his ears. He thought he was being set up, so he tested the theory by drinking a soda. Once he realized that it was real, he started ordering everything that he could eat and drink. He called his friends and his girlfriend, and before long, he had five people eating with him. Everything that they were eating was going to be placed on his grandson's bill. His girlfriend even questioned him about this; she asked, "Why are you inflicting this bill on your innocent grandson?" He was so excited and self-absorbed that he proudly proclaimed that his future grandson would have the money to take care of the bill. After this, the young man and his crew continued to order and eat as much as they could. They were even abrasive towards their waitress. Finally, the dishwasher walked over to the guy and said that the manager wanted to see him. Nevertheless, he was too intoxicated and entitled to stand to his feet, so the manager finally made his way to their table. The manager held onto a small handmade book, and he said, "Mr. Denison, this book has been with me for over two decades. You can have this." After this, he ripped a page out of the book and handed it to the young man. On the paper was listed 700 bottles of beer and a list of other food items that had been eaten in excess. "What is this?" the young man asked as the life seemed to drain from his face. "This is your grandfather's bill," stated the manager. The total of the bill was 415,000 naira, which is equivalent to $1,088 American dollars. When the young man looked up, all of his friends and his girlfriend had fled. He'd gone into that restaurant thinking that he was going to eat as much as he could and place the bill on his future grandson, only to discover that his grandfather had already done the same thing to him. So, while his bill would fall on his grandson's head, his grandfather's bill had fallen on his head. This is exactly how witchcraft works.

I remember being a horrible steward when it came to money. I was married and my ex and myself had fallen into the trap of taking a payday loan. These loans have to be repaid on your next payday. Howbeit, when our paydays would roll around, we had so many bills and unplanned expenses that we would pay off the loan and then take another loan. Finally, this wasn't enough, so we went to another cash advance place and got another loan. So, every two weeks, we found ourselves in a vicious cycle of paying off the loans and then rewriting to get another loan. And try as we may, we could never seem to get out of this cycle. While in this loop, we separated and when we did, we both decided to go for broke and just pay off the loans without rewriting. But now having to pay one hundred percent of the bills, I found myself back in the clutches of debt, constantly writing and rewriting for a cash advance. This is what witchcraft looks like. It solves an immediate problem, but creates an even greater problem in the future. Just like getting a loan is the same as borrowing from your future, playing with witchcraft is asking a demonic entity to help you to solve an immediate problem, answer a plaguing question or satisfy an unquenchable lust now, and the familial spirit who answered that person's petition would be able to collect its debt in the future. In truth, many people today are paying for their grandparents' choices. The Bible says that a good man leaves an inheritance for his children and his children's children. Considering this, what does a bad man leave to his children and grandchildren? Debt, of course! And when the debt falls on the head of a generation, we see a lot of premature deaths, alcoholism, perversion, divorces, mental illnesses and every evil under the sun. What this does is it sends that generation in a frenzy looking for answers and solutions. Satan then strategically places people in their lives to introduce them to paganism and witchcraft. What is he doing? Getting them to renew the contract, of course!

And get this—we see a lot of people returning to witchcraft today because of what's being popularized in Hollywood. They see airbrushed and Photoshopped pictures of men and women; they see wealth and what appears to be perfection. This causes them to become unrealistic and unreasonable. What this means is, you'll find a lot of women who are unintentionally sabotaging their relationships because of something they saw on the big screen. The same is true for men. Consequently, they end up getting their hearts broken. Being immature and not knowing how to handle rejection, they eventually find themselves dabbling with witchcraft. What they've just done is resigned the contracts that their grandparents and/or ancestors failed to pay off. This ensnares more generations; that is, until someone within that family structure wakes up and confronts all of those demonic systems. This is why we see the reemergence of sage, the popularizing of chakras and a host of demonic practices. We are all spirits, and because of this, we are spiritual! This is why we need the Holy Spirit to guide us. Without Him, we'll find ourselves looking for answers from fallen angels. These demons can't save themselves. Why would they know the answer to our life's problems? They don't. They just pacify an immediate need in exchange for our children and grandchildren. In truth, if many of the people out there who've lost loved ones prematurely, especially to an act of violence, were to understand demonic contracts, they would pray over all of their children, renouncing all claims to them that could be made by Satan and his henchmen. But again, most prophetic people don't know who they are! They refer to themselves as "empaths" and go on a mission to discover a higher knowledge of themselves. *This is error!* Matthew 6:33 reads, "But seek ye <u>first</u> the kingdom of God, and his righteousness; and all these things shall be added unto you." And by "first," God isn't saying to call yourself a Christian first, and from there, He'd give us the desires of our hearts. No, He's saying to get saved <u>and</u> put Him before everyone and everything. This takes time! He must be number one in our lives, otherwise, we have erected for ourselves idols. What's amazing is, if you'll look at patterns, you will find that most people who tend to place themselves and others before God almost always find themselves in a string of relationships with narcissistic people. And narcissists specialize in making these people feel worthless without them. All the same, narcissists are professionals at detecting people who have idolatry in their hearts. The reason for this is—again, the spirit behind narcissism is the Jezebel spirit, and Jezebel was an idol worshiper who turned the hearts of Israel away from God. Therefore, wherever you find idolatry, you'll find the Jezebel spirit also known as the common narcissist. And after counseling many empath/narcissist relationships, you'll soon discover that the only way out of these types of structures isn't to convince the narcissist to not be narcissistic, after all, counseling won't turn a devil into an angel. The objective is to get the empath to stop idolizing the narcissist and anything else the empath may be idolizing.

The reemergence of witchcraft is not something that's new unfortunately. Anytime a demonic contract is coming to an end, Satan will go out of his way to get the parties involved to renew that contract. This is because he specializes in legalities; he understands his rights, allowances and restrictions. So, the next time you find yourself in a rough patch, make sure that you are prayerful, that you are fasting and that you resist the temptation to get even with anyone who's hurt you. All the same, don't rush your relationships. The most common witchcraft performed today comes from angry women and men (mostly women) who allowed someone to love bomb them, establish themselves as important fixtures in their lives, and then, promptly exit their lives, but not before hurting and humiliating them. Not knowing how to foster a broken heart, these men and women turned to witchcraft in their attempts to tame, train or get even with the people who broke their hearts. But what they didn't realize was that their children and grandchildren would have to pay for their poor choices. This is what generational curses are made up; they are the results of broken people trying to satisfy an ungodly appetite.

Heal, forgive and move on! Remember, vengeance belongs to God. All the same, also keep in mind that you can't expect

God to "pay back" someone from destroying an ungodly relationship. That's like asking McDonald's to give you a refund on a Whopper that you purchased from Burger King. Thank God for your deliverance and move on!

The Power of No

There are three answers that we have the power and the responsibility to give. They are:

1. Yes
2. No
3. Maybe

You are a self-run kingdom. Your assignment is to integrate your kingdom into God's Kingdom—to submit your kingdom to the Kingdom of God; this way, your personal government mirrors God's government. You are a king or a queen, but Jesus Christ is King of kings and Lord of lords. These three words (yes, no and maybe) are legal terms in your kingdom, just as they are in God's Kingdom. "Yes" is a permissive word; it allows people (and spirits) to exercise certain behaviors in areas of your life that they ordinarily wouldn't be able to operate in. "No" is a restricting word; it prohibits people (and spirits) from entering areas of your life or exercising certain behaviors in your life at any given time. It also renders their behavior illegal should they operate outside of your permission. Maybe is a neutral term; it stalls a person's progress until you have given that person further notice. Let's go back to the waiting room example. Again, the conscious mind is the waiting room of the soul. It is here where we weigh the words that we hear; it is here that we decide what to allow into our hearts and what to cast down. Anytime we attach the word "yes" to anything sitting in those waiting rooms, whatever we said "yes" to then rises up and enters our subconscious, where it burrows itself in our hearts. Out of the heart flows the issues of life, and out of the abundance of the heart, the mouth speaks. Again, the heart is the epicenter of our souls. This is why the word "no" is important. We have to study so that whenever a thought invades our conscious, we can compare that thought to what we've read and learned. If it is a lie, we can cast it down in the conscious realm. Once it leaves the conscious, it can no longer be cast down; instead, it has to be cast out. It can only be cast down if it is returned to the conscious mind and replaced by truth. And because the word "no," is a legal expression in the natural realm and the spiritual realm, any person or spirit that does not honor this word when it is spoken (whenever it relates to a person and what legally belongs to that person, be it material or spatial), becomes a trespasser the minute that person or spirit goes against the speaker's will. For example, if I told a woman that she could not have my purse, but she took it anyway, in that moment, she has become a trespasser. Now, the word "trespasser" can be expanded to mean many things, including, a thief, a robber, a kidnapper, a murderer, a rapist, a liar, etc. Therefore, a more acceptable term for trespasser would be "criminal." This is why in the ministry of deliverance, it's easy to bind a spirit that is no longer wanted or one that came into or remained in a person's life without having the legal grounds to do so. Sure, demons are the biggest legalists you'll ever come across, but like human criminals, they are known for breaking and entry. If they can find a point of access into a person's life, they will use it. If they're not bound and told to leave, chances are, they won't leave. This is why God said in John 10:1, "Verily, verily, I say unto you, He that entereth not by the door into the sheepfold, but climbeth up some other way, the same is a thief and a robber." The word "door" denotes legal access, but the word "window" denotes illegal access; these are words of protocol.

The word "no" is probably the most hated word in the world, not just the English language. Our parents said no to us, and there were times when we felt like they were ruining our lives by refusing to give us whatever it was that we wanted or by restricting us from doing whatever it was that we wanted to do. We cried, we yelled and we threatened to run away from home. We did everything within our power to bend our parents' wills, but thankfully, most of them didn't budge. For the people whose parents did give in the majority of the time, your experience was different, which ultimately means that your perspective is different or was different. If you were able to easily manipulate your parents, chances are, you are a narcissist or you have been narcissistic at some point; that is, if you haven't gone through deliverance and counseling. I saw the end result of what spoiled children look like and how they reason, and they don't grow up to be happy campers. No. Instead, they grow up to be relatively unreasonable and narcissistic, always expecting the world and everyone in it to cater to their needs. When this doesn't happen, they pass themselves off as victims, even when they are exercising predatory behaviors. Eventually, anger and depression begin to eat away at them because they genuinely feel like the world is mishandling them, and no one is doing his or her part to make them happy. Like I said, they tend to be very unreasonable. Having a conversation with a person like this is surreal because of the way they see life. For example, I've had conversations with narcissists that sounded like this:

> **Narcissist:** She wants me to help around *her* house!
> **Me:** You live there, don't you? Rent free, at that. Why wouldn't you want to help out?
> **Narcissist:** I'm not her personal maid! I'm grateful for her letting me stay here; don't get me wrong, but I didn't sign up to be her maid!
> **Me:** Okay. Start giving her some money on the rent and utilities then.
> **Narcissist:** Girl … (Silence)
> **Me:** No! You can't have it both ways. If you were staying with me, you'd be helping to clean my house and you'd be paying half the bills. And if I caught you talking about me while living under my roof, I'd put you out.
> **Narcissist:** That's why I wouldn't live with you.

If someone opens their house up to you and allows you to lodge there freely, sound reasoning would dictate that you help out as much as you can and you show some gratitude, even if you don't fully agree with that person's lifestyle or rules. I'd be cooking, cleaning, helping the children with their homework and walking the dog or changing the cat's litter (if they had pets). But narcissists don't see life through this lens. Anyone who's helping them out, in their eyes, is doing their due diligence. In their warped opinions, they don't owe those people anything, including a "thank you." Instead, they'll cough up some foolish reason as to why they believe that person is "supposed" to help them out. They are very entitled people who think everyone is their personal "ram in the bush." They are the types of people who go into companies, pay a bill and when the cashier accidentally overpays them while giving them their change, they'll leave with the money and brag about how God blessed them. They don't consider the fact that the cashier may lose her job. They are the types of people who'll cause car accidents and then thank God that the cars that crashed into one another narrowly missed them. They don't care about the people who got hurt (or worse) in those car accidents. To them, those people were pawns in a larger game. They are the types of people who mistreat and mishandle other people, but when those people react negatively or express disdain for the way they've been treated, narcissists will typically see themselves as saints suffering persecution for Christ's sake. They'll post up and preach about their haters, because they genuinely feel like the people they've provoked should have just accepted their abusive treatment. If you said to a narcissist, "She told me that you cursed her out first, and that's why she cursed you out," the narcissist would probably respond with something like, "I did because I was frustrated! Do you know what kind of week I've been having?! She knows my situation!" After this, the narcissist would detail a long list of reasons as to why he or she feels that he or she was allowed to curse at the other person, followed by another list of reasons as to why the other person should have just given the narcissist what he or she wanted and just walked away. Again, they are very unrealistic and unreasonable in regards to how they see the world and everyone in it.

"No" is a delivering word. Most of us have lost friends just because we told them "no" or we've watched relationships fall apart simply because we said "no" to the person we were romantically linked to. And get this, the word "no" was designed to test the heart, maturity and spirit of a man! As I mentioned earlier, I have estranged family members simply because I have rules in my life that they are not willing to abide by. And get this, I'm perfectly okay with this! You have to absolutely love some folks from a distance. I actually prefer that we keep our distance from one another for now because I know what a relationship with them looks like. It has to be a toxic relationship, complete with weekly arguments, threats, name-calling and more. There's no getting around this. Check out this dialogue to understand my point:

> "I'm going to cheat on you, no matter what you say!"
> "But you're my husband! I can't be with a cheating man!"

"I hear you, but that's just who I am! I'm going to continue seeing other people! Take it or leave it!"

"I'll leave it, but I won't leave you! I'm calling our pastor, your mother and a counselor to address this!"

"For what? I'm still going to cheat!"

This is obviously a dialogue between a philandering husband and his desperate wife. The man is being honest with his wife. He's made a decision to be a cheater. He's unrepentant, and he loves the sin he's in. Nevertheless, the wife is convinced that she can force him to be faithful to her, so she's planning to bring their pastor, a counselor and her mother-in-law into the discussion, hoping that one of them will have enough power and influence in the man's life to convince or force him to be monogamous. This is similar to a conversation, for example, with my family members. If I say, "No smoking, fighting, cursing, or having sex in my house," they have to abide by this. Howbeit, if a family member comes to my house, for example, and lights up a cigarette, that family member is pretty much having a similar dialogue with me as the philandering husband had with his wife. That family member is telling me that he or she is not going to honor my rules. In other words, that family member is saying "no" to my established rules. That family member is saying "no" to my "no." This puts the ball in my court. It would be unreasonable for me to invite this person back into my home or my life, and then, proceed to complain about him or her violating my rules. No. Instead, the minute the person violates my house rules, that person loses his or her access to my house; the minute a person violates my life's rules, that person loses privileges in my life, and if that person continues to violate my boundaries, that person then loses access to my life. These are the only options! Anything beyond this is witchcraft! You can't control the will of another human being, so if someone makes it very clear that they are going to go beyond every "no" and boundary you establish, this is when you have to exercise your established penalties. A penalty for smoking a cigarette in my house would probably be a rebuke the first time, but the second time, that person would be banned from coming to my house. This means that I said "no," but now, I'm enforcing that restriction without apology. Yes, even at the expense of losing some relationships. Get this—the word "no" keeps the devil in the waiting room. He's an impatient creature, so he'll go looking for another point of access. There are many benefits to the word "no," which includes:

1. No creates boundaries around what's important to you, meaning, you get to keep what's important to you.

2. No drives the wrong people out of your life. People who truly love and respect you won't be offended or driven out of your life just because you have boundaries in place that they have to honor. The right people will give you the grace and the space to say no. The wrong ones will try to make you feel guilty or humiliated whenever you say no to them.

3. You preserve time by saying no.

4. You preserve space by saying no.

5. You preserve energy by saying no.

6. You preserve your sanity by saying no.
7. You save money by saying no.
8. Saying no helps to build and maintain your confidence.
9. Saying no protects you and your family from predatory people.
10. Saying no to others teaches your children to respect your no whenever you say it to them.
11. Saying no helps you to remain in control of your life.
12. Saying no to the wrong things and the wrong people is the same as saying yes to the right ones.

Every boundary has benefits, but the most important benefit of them all is peace. Whenever a system is uninterrupted, that system will produce whatever it was designed to produce without delay. There are many blessings that God has availed to you and for you, but in order to receive these blessings, you have to draw lines of demarcation around yourself and you have to enforce those boundaries. This teaches you to respect yourself, and it teaches others to respect you as well. People who have sound and solid boundaries around themselves that they enforce without apology are often surrounded by sound and reasonable people who, not only respect their boundaries, but these people have boundaries of their own. Never trust someone who doesn't have solid boundaries in their lives; in other words, don't trust people who have fluid boundaries. Please note:

1. Wealthy people have boundaries.

2. Successful people have boundaries.
3. Sane people have boundaries.

You will never find a person who's built anything great, be it a family, a business or a reputation without having set and enforced a bunch of boundaries—boundaries that cost them some pretty valuable relationships. Understand that a large number of people will distance themselves from you the moment you stop allowing your boundaries to be violated. But that's okay. This is what your boundaries were designed to do; they were put in place to protect the integrity of every system in your life. Your boundaries are designed to protect you and everything/everyone you love! People build families that are emotionally, spiritually, mentally, financially, physically and socially strong by placing boundaries around their families and enforcing them. If you want to be married, practice saying the word "no." If you want a happy marriage, practice saying the word "no." If you want any measure of success, practice saying the word "no." If you want peace on every side, practice saying the word "no." And finally, practice enforcing it.

TUG-OF-WAR (WHEN HEAVEN AND HELL PULL ON YOUR POTENTIAL)

Genesis 1:1-4: In the beginning God created the heaven and the earth. And the earth was without form, and void; and darkness was upon the face of the deep. And the Spirit of God moved upon the face of the waters. And God said, Let there be light: and there was light. And God saw the light, that it was good: and God divided the light from the darkness.

God created mankind in the same manner that He created the Earth. Let's look at this scripture another way. In the beginning, God created man and woman. And the man was without form (he was a pile of dust), and void (absent of life and light or, better yet, revelation), and darkness was upon the face of the man's potential. And God moved upon the man's potential and said, "Let there be life, and there was life. And God saw the living man, and he was good. And God took the man, who was now a being of light, and placed him in the Garden of Eden, separating him from all that was evil. From there, God brought the woman out of the man, thus, pulling out a measure of his potential. He then continued to publish His systems with mankind, and all of these systems were and are surrounded by a single boundary. That boundary is and was His Word. Within that boundary, God began to teach the man to pull on and pull out his potential.

The more he tilled the garden (his flesh), the more he would manifest his potential. Nevertheless, the woman who'd been pulled out of the man represented a measure of the man's potential as well. Man had the potential to do good, just as he had the potential to do evil and become evil. Potential is a two-sided coin. This is why one day, the woman wandered off towards the edge of the Garden. Letting curiosity get the best of her, she began to look at the many trees, taking fruits from the ones she passed by. She marveled at how delicious each unique fruit was. She then looked at the Tree of the Knowledge of Good and Evil, and for a moment, she allowed her imaginations to get the best of her. She wandered closer to the tree, admiring its beauty and marveling at its height. That's when a voice came from behind her. "Did God actually say, 'You shall not eat of any tree in the garden?'" Startled, she looked behind her and saw a snake. She'd caught Satan's eye from a distance. Seeing her potential, he'd made his way towards her, hoping to strike up a conversation. It worked! Shortly thereafter, the woman crossed her very first boundary and entered into sin. Again, this is a fictitious and exaggerated account of what happened that ominous day in the Garden of Eden.

Let's look at two homophones (words that sound the same but have different meanings) "wonder" and "wander." The following definitions were taken from Merriam Webster.
- **Wonder:** to feel curiosity or doubt.
- **Wander:** to move about without a fixed course, aim, or goal.

The word "wonder" deals with the head, but the word "wander" deals with the body. Whatever you put your mind on, your body will follow. For example, whenever I'm walking my dog, he will occasionally fixate on something or someone. When he does this, his feet slowly, but surely turn in the direction of what he's fixating on. In most cases, he'll redirect his focus and his feet will follow, meaning, he simply wondered then wandered for a second, but not long enough for me to have to pull on his leash. There are times, of course, when I do have to give him a slight nudge; then again, there have been times when I've had to pull on his leash because he was downright determined to get to something or someone. All the same, there are some people who've pet him in the past, so whenever he sees them, he throws all caution to the wind. From there, he happily jogs toward them with me in tow. I don't always pull him away when the people start making their way towards him as well. Whenever his mind is on anything, whether it be a fire hydrant or a person, his body starts heading in that direction. Any and every living thing is wired this way. Whatever we focus on, we follow. Why do you think that Satan bombards you with so many desires and lusts? Why do you think he tempts you? Why do you think that you've attracted so many narcissists? There's a trait in the narcissist that you are likely attracted to and vice versa. So, even when you're trying to avoid narcissistic people, because your mind is still focused on the narcissist you got away from or the concept of narcissism as a whole, you find yourself reconciling with that same spirit in a different body. This is because you keep breaking up with the people, but you haven't broken up with the Satanic system itself. This answers the age-old question, "Why do I only seem to attract a specific type of person?" You attract what you can relate to. These people come your way because hell as noticed your potential. Consider the story of the ex and the pickup truck that I shared in Book One. In short, I'd broken up with the guy and he'd come to my house and attempted to kidnap me. This was after I so foolishly got into his truck with him, hoping that I could convince him to leave me alone. He wasn't the last narcissist that I found myself romantically entangled with. Amazingly enough, I ended up running on foot again from another man who was hellbent on taming me, but this time, it was the middle of the night and I was married to that man! Like the ex, he was driving and trying to catch me while I was trying to get away. This happened after he'd physically assaulted me, dragged me to our bedroom, took my cell phone away, ripped the house phone's cord out of the wall and threatened to kill me if I'd left the bedroom. Like I'd done years prior to that, I'd waited a few minutes, and when I saw an opportunity to get away, I took it—on foot! Do you see the correlation? I kept breaking up with people, and not breaking up with the mindset that attracted those people! Why did I attract folks who thought I needed to be tamed? Because potential is a two-sided coin; that's why! My mother was super empathic, but she'd allowed herself to be ahab'ed or controlled by narcissistic people all her life. I had that same gift of empathy, and I had the potential to be a weapon for the kingdom of darkness (obviously). I was broken and bound.

All the same, I had Godly potential. I had the potential to do a lot of damage to Satan's kingdom if I were to get saved. So, Heaven pulled on my potential, but hell staked claim to it. In other words, this fight was a spiritual one, but I was too carnal to know it. The biggest, most prevalent threat that Satan saw in me was my anointing. This was an anointing that had passed through my father's family generation after generation. On the other hand, the biggest, most prevalent threat that these guys saw in me was my ability to walk away. You see, Jezebelic or narcissistic people don't mind you ending a relationship with them when they know they have you under their influence. This is because even when they walk away, they still have you. So, whenever they decide that they want to revisit the relationship, they know you'll avail yourself to them. Howbeit, I was too broken to stay attached to anyone. Remember, wherever your head or thoughts are, that's where your feet will go. I had an overactive imagination. I never stopped believing that I deserved better than what I had. I'm not saying that I was entitled or difficult to satisfy because I honestly wasn't. The problem was, there was a seed in me that Heaven had sown, and it had already started growing its roots underneath the surface of my heart. My great-grandmother had watered that seed before she'd left the Earth, so whenever I found myself in a toxic relationship, something in me told me that I deserved better. I just couldn't (knowingly) settle down with a toxic person. This is where my head was, so I kept wandering out of relationships in my quest to find myself. When I was in the world, I discovered that this part of my personality put me in eminent danger whenever I paired myself up with the wrong people. (This is part of what made me run to Jesus). This didn't mean that I was cold and heartless; the problem was that all the hell I'd been through as a child had only served to strengthen (and) numb me. In other words, trauma had triggered a different type of response in me. Remember, when two chemicals come together, they produce a specific reaction and whenever you break the breaker, you activate his or her anointing. Anytime I paired up with a narcissist, rage and murder would start bubbling up within that person. And the fact that I didn't know how to bridle my tongue made matters worse. All the same, the fact that I refused to be intimidated and controlled made me the perfect candidate for a missing person's flier. What I didn't realize was that hell was pulling on my potential; these were the seeds that Satan had sown into me through generational strongholds and the seeds he'd sown into me through trauma. Nevertheless, Heaven was also pulling on my potential. For example, when I was in the sixth grade, I was a pretty decent writer and illustrator. I sat next to the class clown named Michael, and he was an amazing illustrator. I was quiet; he was not. Whenever I drew something, I'd show it to him, and he'd grab the paper and start adding details to it. I learned a lot from him, even though he was always getting himself into trouble. Our teacher (Mrs. Alexander) was considered the meanest teacher in the school. Most people did not want to take her class because she rarely smiled, plus, she was known for paddling students and kicking them out of her class. All the same, she wasn't the type of teacher who'd tell a student to stop doing something; instead, she'd immediately reprimand that student. So, it goes without saying that I made it a point to stay on her good side.

One day, Mrs. Alexander told us that she had to grade papers. We'd heard this speech before. She was going to give us a few minutes to get a book off one of the shelves or find something to keep us busy before we had to return to our seats. After that, we could not utter a word or make a sound. I loved those moments. They gave me time to write fictional stories or read a book. On this particular day, I decided to write my version of a paperback book. What I would do was take some loose-leaf paper and fold it in half. I'd then staple the spine, draw an image on the cover and write a title for the book. From there, I'd proceed to write a horror story. Like many times before, I sat there and wrote a pretty lengthy story. I don't remember how or why Mrs. Alexander got her hands on my book, but she did, and she loved it. She asked me to come up to her desk, and when I did, she told me that I was an amazing writer. She also told me that I was going to be an author someday. No one had ever said those words to me. Again, Heaven was pulling on my potential. Mrs. Alexander asked me if I had more books I'd written. I did. They were in my backpack. I took them out and brought them up to her desk. She then asked if she could keep them. I excitedly said yes. She put my books in a small box (or maybe a crate, I don't remember) right next to her desk. So, every time we had "quiet time," I'd write another book. I even started writing books at home just so I could give them to Mrs. Alexander because she kept watering my potential with compliments. Before long, the box was nearly full of books with drawings on the front. If that wasn't enough, during some quiet times, many of the students would walk up to Mrs. Alexander's desk to get one of my books to read. I was so taken aback that I didn't know what to say.

One day, Mrs. Alexander decided that she wanted to have a parent-teacher conference with my parents because she believed in me so much that she couldn't stop talking about my books and how I'd be a famous author someday. My mother ended up coming to the school, and while on one hand, I was happy, on the other hand, I was terrified. This is because we were poor and I knew my mother was going to focus on the fact that I was using paper she'd bought me for school to write my books. I was right. Mrs. Alexander excitedly told my mother about my gift. I don't remember what she said to my mother, I just remember that my mom was in no ways happy about what she saw—a box FULL of paper she'd purchased that I'd converted into books. What I do remember is that Mrs. Alexander was trying to get my mother to pay attention to my gift; maybe even put me in some programs to grow it. But my mother could not stop focusing on how much money I'd thrown away by drawing and writing on all that paper. Realizing that my mother was missing the big picture, Mrs. Alexander ended the meeting. I wasn't in the room for that part. In truth, I don't think my mother verbally said anything about her being upset about me wasting paper; I think my teacher saw this in her eyes. Of course, I got in trouble, and I'd reasoned within myself that my writing days were over. The next day (or the next Monday; I don't remember), Mrs. Alexander walked up to me while I was working on an assignment she'd given us. She then handed me a large stack of typing paper. She didn't say anything about my mother or her response. She just told me that she didn't want me to stop writing. She handed me a lot of typing paper and told me that when I ran out of it, I could come to her desk and get as much as I needed. When I looked in her eyes, I didn't see the mean woman everyone said she was. I saw a fighter. Mrs. Alexander was one of the first apostolic gifts I'd come in contact with, and Heaven used her to pull on my potential. And let me say this. My mother wasn't being a bad mother; she was just limited in how she saw the world. I was always running out of paper, and she was working two jobs. She only responded the way she knew how to respond. There were no authors in my family. She couldn't "see" me becoming who Mrs. Alexander said I'd become, and that's quite alright. Not everyone will see your potential, not even your parents. Remember this—God will only allow certain people to see snippets of what He's placed in you. Typically, these people have an assignment to water one or more of those seeds. All the same, the prayers of my paternal great-grandmother were still covering me, even though she'd passed away when I was six-years old. I still remembered going to church with her; I still remembered spending a lot of time at her house. She was a praying woman who loved and feared the Lord. When she'd transitioned out of this Earth, her prayers were still covering me. So, eventually my potential began to wake up. I started getting curious about God, and I'd occasionally pray to Him, especially when I was in trouble. In other words, I began to wonder. Eventually, I wandered into a church and got saved. Nevertheless, after I got saved, I kept wandering around in the world because it was all I knew. It took years for me to fully surrender to God.

In the beginning, God created you, but darkness was on the face of your potential. God then planted seeds in your heart, but once He planted you in the Earth, Satan went out of his way to bury what God had planted. He caused hurt people to hurt you, he lied to you repeatedly and he used you to hurt others. This was so that he could sow the seeds of rejection, abandonment, trauma, neglect, hopelessness, idolatry, and sexual immorality into you. And then, the race was on. Satan sent people your way to water the seeds he'd sown, and God sent people your way to water the seeds He'd sown. Sometimes, these were people you met in passing, and in many instances, they were the romantic interests who you gave a measure of your land (attention and time) to. What and who you are today is a product of the people who've been watering those seeds in your life. If you have chosen a life of sin; trust me, the enemy has used a LOT of people to water the seeds he's sown, all the while, God has to send a person here and there to water a few seeds at a time. Like the Garden of Eden, both of these seeds took root, and before long, you had good trees and bad trees. If sin was the dominant craving in your life, you kept eating from the wrong trees (systems), while Satan commanded you not to eat from the good ones. When you ate from the good ones, he punished you. How? By using the folks he'd stationed in your life. This is why every time you try to, for example, go back to college, write a book, start a business or do anything productive, someone in your family or in your life suddenly started distracting you. It could be that best friend of yours who called you crying uncontrollably about her philandering boyfriend. You had to stop what you were doing to comfort and hang out with her. After your "virtue" was gone, she went back and reconciled with her boyfriend while you went back to life as normal. Your interest in writing the book, launching the business, filing a trademark or doing whatever you were excited about doing was suddenly demoted to a fading idea —something you planned to get around to whenever you could. You didn't realize that Satan had used a common tactic or wile of his to steal your virtue (strength, inspiration) from you. Or maybe, the moment you started writing the book, you met some guy. As a writing teacher, I've seen several of my students get taken out this way! I always warn my classes about the sudden reemergence of an ex whenever they're writing. This usually indicates that there is a door still opened in the realm of the spirit that needed to be closed. You can't imagine how disappointed I've been every time I've watched one of my students fall into the trap of entertaining one of the weapons that had been formed against them. And within days or a couple of weeks (I teach a five week course; let that sink in), they'd be too distracted to finish their books. Of course, they'd started entertaining or dating these people again, and Satan will have successfully locked them back in to the realm of mediocrity. A few months later (in most cases), they'd be single again, and their interest in finishing their books would be pretty much nonexistent. You have to remember that every time Heaven pulls on your potential, hell will feel that movement! Satan will then throw fiery darts (people) at you to offend, scare or date you; whichever method is needed to bring you back under his control.

Another example I'd like to share is of another woman who'd impacted my life majorly. Again, this was someone who came off as a "meanie." First and foremost, when I was a child, I had been surrounded by sexual perversion. I was immersed in it! So, it goes without saying that as a young woman, the seeds of seduction and fornication had already started producing fruit in my life. I dressed seductively, hung around seductive women and lived a lifestyle that was completely antithetical to the design God had given me. So again, the seeds Satan had sown were thriving in my life. Nevertheless, Heaven wasn't ready to give up on me. This time, the person God used was a woman I'd worked with; she was a manager over me for about a year, and in that small window of time, I saw something I'd never seen before—a chaste woman! Every woman I knew was in survivor's mode, but to see someone who abstained from premarital sex and truly loved the Lord—someone who was not running around using a lot of religious quotes to cover her hypocrisy, but a woman who was actually living what she preached was a wonder within itself! I saw what I could become; I saw my potential on display! In other words, she didn't realize it, but she was a God-sent activator! And if that wasn't enough, I remember her extending trust and favor to me. She knew my lifestyle! She knew that I loved to hang out with my friends, drink, party and engage in premarital sex. Why then would she hand me her paycheck and tell me to deposit it into her account just about every payday? This is a small deed for some, but for me, it was major. I've never been a thief before (save the time when I was around twelve. I'd acted as an accomplice a couple of times when a friend of mine stole junk food from a store.) Believe it or not, that little act was major for me. I was unsaved, but relatively trustworthy, and rather than focus on what was wrong with me, she keyed in on one of my strengths. Why would she take time out to even rebuke me about the clothes I wore to work? Some people would have gotten offended, but I didn't. This is because she was the first Christian I'd met who truly acted like Christ. I genuinely didn't mind her correcting me because it didn't feel like judgment. It felt different. I believe this is because she didn't just talk about Christ, she lived for Him! She didn't preach at me a lot, but her lifestyle spoke longer and louder than her words. Whenever she criticized some of the clothes I wore to work, I didn't get angry like I'd done with other women. I didn't think she was "jealous" or "insecure." This is because she could see me—and by me, I don't mean the physical Tiffany. She saw who I was underneath it all, and for a young woman, THIS IS IMPORTANT! When she critiqued me about my clothes, I would just smile and try to defend what I was wearing in a joking manner. I truly loved and admired her because she didn't incorporate a "hallelujah" or a "thank you, Jesus" in her discussions with me (like a few hypocrites had done). Instead, she spoke to me and not at me. No manipulation. No fluff. No filters. Eventually, she was transferred to another store, but it was too late; for Satan, that is. Some new seeds had been sown, and some old seeds had been watered. Not long after that, I got saved. She helped to put my mind on Christ, and one day, I wandered into a church. Three services later, I mustered up enough courage to get out of my seat and answer the call to salvation. And that's when I entered the greatest fight of my life. I can tell you stories upon stories of exes who didn't want to let go after our relationship had ended, but none of those stories can even slightly mirror the fight that I found myself in once I said yes to Christ. I learned that Satan is the craziest ex anyone could ever have. He'd sown too many seeds and used too many of his resources to just watch all his work go down the drain, so he pursued me like he pursues most empaths—with vigor! Nevertheless, God kept me and extended grace to me. Grace allows you the space to fall while you grow, and that I did a lot of. Like a toddler learning to walk, a new Christian will stumble and fall as he or she tries to find him or herself. I didn't get saved and come straightway out of sexual immorality; when I got saved, my tongue didn't follow me immediately. Nevertheless, God continued to send people my way to water what He'd put in me. All the same, He protected me from religious, judgmental people by making me unappealing to them and vice versa.

What about you? Please know that you are a walking and talking spirit wrapped in dust. Underneath that dust, there is potential. You have a measure of reach that would allow you to pull out a snippet of your own potential, even if you're unsaved. In Hollywood, we see unsaved folks who once pulled on their own gifts and talents, eventually revealing an extension of themselves to the world. Over time, they found other people to pull on their potential—people who had a greater reach. It goes without saying that those people couldn't heal, save or deliver them; they could only pull on their potential. Similarly, you have potential buried under your pain, your pride, your fears and your rejection. And every time you soul tie yourself with another person, you stack another body on top of that potential, making it more and more difficult for you to pull it out. This is why God incorporates leaders into the equation. Jeremiah 3:15 reads, "And I will give you pastors according to mine heart, which shall feed you with knowledge and understanding." These shepherds are the Moses' who God uses to lead you out of one mindset and into another. And as they lead you, God uses them to pull on your potential, but remember this—they can pull on your potential, but only you can pull it out. All the same, God will send people to sprinkle a little water on your potential, just as He'll send people to pour on your potential. This gives us a whole new view of Malachi 3:10, which reads, "Bring ye all the tithes into the storehouse, that there may be meat in mine house, and prove me now herewith, saith the LORD of hosts, if I will not open you the windows of heaven, and pour you out a blessing, that there shall not be room enough to receive it." I've learned that this pour God speaks of comes in the form of earthen vessels, but please hear me when I say that you have to submit in order to receive the pour. All the same, you have to honor the people God sends to pour into you, and if you've had issues with authority figures before, I admonish you to pray away that fear of authority because Satan will use an event from your past to get you to reject the pour needed to water your future. He'll make you suspicious of the people, make you question their love for you or make you question their faith walk. And of course, his favorite tool to use is offense. Broken people are easily offended because they see life and people through a warped perspective.

What's underneath the hurt, the rejection, the insecurities and the perversions is a treasure unlike anything that has ever been seen before on the face of this Earth. Deep within the pits of your heart are the answers to so many people's prayers. But potential is like an egg; it has to be fertilized before it can come to life. Unfortunately, there are so many people in the world and in the church who've been hurt by authority figures, and because of their experiences, it's hard for them to trust anyone who attempts to lead them. Consequently, they try to walk "with" their leaders, rather than following them as they follow Christ. In other words, they sabotage every relationship that is designed to pull them out of the darkness and into God's plans for them. They feel the need to be on the same level as their leaders and mentors, and this births familiarity. When a person becomes too familiar with his or her leader, especially if that person is immature in the faith, that individual will start trying to lead the leader, and in many cases, even control the leader. If you want to go to the next level in Christ, you can't engage in this type of behavior! Being led by another human being may be completely foreign to you or uncomfortable for you, but this is something you have to personally wrestle to the ground so that God can deliver you from the strongholds that Satan has used to ensnare you. This allows someone else the ability to pull on your potential, and once it begins to surface, God will allow you to fully pull it out. In 1 Corinthians 3:6, Apostle Paul said, "I have planted, Apollos watered; but God gave the increase." In short, there is power in community. In other words, you can't do this alone. You can only pull so much of your potential out, but God will use people who have a greater reach than you to pull on your potential; that is, until they unearth it. From there, God will allow you to pull it out. Think of archaeologists. Their job is to dig the dirt and go into the caves, excavating the ground, and then pull out the treasures that would have otherwise remain buried. And these treasures include gold coins, clothing, documents and other historical artifacts. Then again, there is the miner. A miner's job is to dig the dirt as well, but when he does this, he's looking for coal, ore and other minerals that are typically found in the Earth. You need:

- **the Archaeologist:** these are the people God will use to pull out the generational gifts and talents that somehow got buried over time. These are typically the people you meet in passing, like my former teacher (Mrs. Alexander) or the assistant manager who I worked under. Once their jobs are done, they have to move on because they are not necessarily designed to be permanent fixtures in your life.

- **the Miner:** this is the apostolic gift who God will use to blow some things up in your life. This may be your pastor or it could be someone who speaks into your life, for example, at a conference or an event. This person is not afraid to offend or lose you because he or she is more focused on what's in you than how you feel. Believe it or not, most people who've come across miners got offended and walked away from them because, for example, they were prophetically instructed by those miners to end relationships, repent of a behavior or sow a seed, not realizing that the miner was directly attacking idolatry in their lives. This is what Jesus did with the rich young ruler who asked Him, "Master, what must I do to inherit eternal life?" Jesus told him to go and sell everything that he owned, and then, follow Him. Jesus was challenging a system in his life, but the young man had become a slave to that system. Of course, Jesus was both an archaeologist and a miner, but in this particular encounter, He served as a miner. The Bible tells us that the young man walked away grieved. People still do this today, especially if they are instructed to sow a seed. My strongest suit was that I absolutely REFUSED to get offended with the people who God sent to throw bombs at some of my patterns of thinking. Even when I was unsaved, I made it a point to honor them to the best of my ability. I have my mother to thank for this because I watched her honor authority figures over the course of my life! Now granted, she did tolerate some people she shouldn't have tolerated, but even up until her death, she always referred to her elders as "ma'am" and "sir." She had a solid heart of honor.

- **the Planter:** these are God's hired workers. Think about a farmer. He may hire some people to plant seeds on his farm; these people are not full-time employees. They are less than seasonal; they are contractual, meaning, once their job is done, they have to move on. These are the people who God will use to speak into your life. Many of these people are folks you'll meet in passing, but the difference between them and the archaeologists is that their jobs are completed a lot faster. It takes an archaeologist a while to dig; this is because they are unearthing something that's been buried. But the planter is not burying or unearthing anything; his or her job is just to sow a seed and move on. Now, whether that seed takes root or not is entirely up to you.
- **the Tiller (Cultivator):** this is normally your pastor.

Please understand that a tiller (machine) rips through the dirt in order to pull out the dirt's potential. And this has to be done often in certain seasons. This is why you can't allow yourself to get offended or remain offended with your leaders, as challenging as this may be! Satan will always try to separate you from the tillers in your life because they have access to something he wants—your soul (mind, will, emotions). He's staked claim to your soul, so to him, they are intruding upon his territory. And the greatest machine or mechanism he has is called offense! You see, we love our pastors when they till certain areas, but when they hit the rejection underneath the surface or the perversion hiding in the midst of our gardens, the spirit of offense rises up to protect Satan's investment. The spirits of offense and pride are "guarding spirits." Their job is to protect or guard something that Satan has planted. Nevertheless, offensive thoughts have potential in them! On one hand, whenever we're offended, we're tempted to walk away from our tillers and stay far away from them. On the other hand, if we are to take that offense and hand it to God, pledging that we won't mismanage our relationships with our pastors, God will then take that offense and give us what's called understanding. Understanding is the shovel that allows us to plow through offense and pull the revelation out of it! The way this looks is, every time an event happens where you find yourself offended, that event isolates itself in your memory bank, along with whatever beliefs, thoughts or patterns (strongholds) that Satan is trying to protect; it's a seed that's trying to take root. And in order for that offense to grow fruits, it has to protect itself by growing a hard outer shell called pride. And like any other seed, offense has to be watered. In other words, the egg needs to be fertilized. When Satan successfully implants offense in your heart, he will then start sending people to agree with your offense. For example, pay attention to the folks on your job and at your church. You'll notice that the people who are the most rebellious against leadership tend to clot together. If you, in turn, get offended with the leadership, those people will all of a sudden start speaking to you and wanting to hang out with you. This is just Satan's attempt to fertilize that seed! But if you commit to honoring your leaders and commit to fighting for your relationship with them, despite what you feel, and if you ask the Holy Spirit to help you to get past the offense, God responds, not by changing how you feel, but by giving you a new perspective. This is another vantage point, meaning, He will take you to another height to give you a different view of the situation and your leaders. And get this—there will be times when you're wrong and there will be times when they are wrong, but you have to commit to honoring them and humbling yourself. This isn't easy; no one said it would be! Most of us are so used to having short-term relationships that whenever we come in contact with the tillers, we run away screaming bloody church hurt because we're afraid of what's on the other side of the event, not realizing that Satan orchestrated the offense because he saw our potential starting to peek through.

- **the Farmer:** believe it or not, this is you. You have to humble yourself and repeatedly turn the ground (flesh) until what's in you begins to surface. And you have to partner with all of the people who God sends in your life to do so. Understand that plowing the flesh is a painful, frustrating and never-ending process, but it gets easier as you "grow along."

And lastly, please know that some of the folks who've hurt you weren't necessarily sent by Satan to water the seeds Satan planted. Some of the craziest people I've met over the course of my life ended up chasing me to Christ or driving me closer to Him. God can and does use bad people to pull the potential out of a person, a movement or an organization. Need evidence? Let's look at a few scriptures.

Judges 14:1-4: And Samson went down to Timnath, and saw a woman in Timnath of the daughters of the Philistines. And he came up, and told his father and his mother, and said, I have seen a woman in Timnath of the daughters of the Philistines: now therefore get her for me to wife. Then his father and his mother said unto him, Is there never a woman among the daughters of thy brethren, or among all my people, that thou goest to take a wife of the uncircumcised

Philistines? And Samson said unto his father, Get her for me; for she pleaseth me well. But his father and his mother knew not that it was of the LORD, that he sought an occasion against the Philistines: for at that time the Philistines had dominion over Israel.

1 Kings 22:15-23: And the king said unto him, Micaiah, shall we go against Ramothgilead to battle, or shall we forbear? And he answered him, Go, and prosper: for the LORD shall deliver it into the hand of the king. And the king said unto him, How many times shall I adjure thee that thou tell me nothing but that which is true in the name of the LORD? And he said, I saw all Israel scattered upon the hills, as sheep that have not a shepherd: and the LORD said, These have no master: let them return every man to his house in peace. And the king of Israel said unto Jehoshaphat, Did I not tell thee that he would prophesy no good concerning me, but evil? And he said, Hear thou therefore the word of the LORD: I saw the LORD sitting on his throne, and all the host of heaven standing by him on his right hand and on his left. And the LORD said, Who shall persuade Ahab, that he may go up and fall at Ramothgilead? And one said on this manner, and another said on that manner. And there came forth a spirit, and stood before the LORD, and said, I will persuade him. And the LORD said unto him, Wherewith? And he said, I will go forth, and I will be a lying spirit in the mouth of all his prophets. And he said, Thou shalt persuade him, and prevail also: go forth, and do so. Now therefore, behold, the LORD hath put a lying spirit in the mouth of all these thy prophets, and the LORD hath spoken evil concerning thee.

If you look throughout the scriptures, you'll see God using unfavorable events and evil people to get Israel to repent. The same is true today. He allows us to make the wrong choices and surround ourselves with the wrong people, and then He'll use those same people to drive us to our knees in prayer and repentance. In other words, He will use them to water the seeds of our potential! Bad people taught me why boundaries are important! They also helped to grow my discernment. Note: discernment is spiritual awareness. It's being familiarized with patterns, whether they are patterns of the eyes (how a seductress looks at a man she's attempting to ensnare) or patterns of behavior. But most importantly, I learned that God loves me; His love is NEVER past tense. The same is true for you. God loves and adores you. Sometimes, it may not feel like He does, and there are times when it will appear that He's forgotten you or is upset with you, none of which are true. Every relationship has highs and lows, including your relationship with Him, but because He's the Most High God, anytime your relationship with Him hits a low place, you or Satan are at fault, not Him. He's consistent; we're not. He will allow you to attract and be traumatized by narcissistic people so that you will be FULLY convinced that He alone is God! All the same, His goal is to get you to start creating solid boundaries in your life. These inflexible boundaries are designed to keep the enemy out; this way, God can pull out your potential. Behind every boundary is a system that the boundary is designed to protect, but when we relax these boundaries and let the wrong folks in, God teaches us the necessity of the boundary by allowing those people to show us the other side of their potential. This is the side that Satan's been watering. He will sometimes allow them to drop seeds that ultimately grow and produce fruit. This teaches us the importance of cultivating our minds and tilling our flesh. This also teaches us why it is NECESSARY for us to guard our hearts. In the end, the goal is for us to produce fruit that gives God the glory and for us to be sold out on Him and Him alone.

Look at every area of your life and ask yourself the following questions:

1. Do I have boundaries in every area of my life?
2. In what area do I keep suffering loss?
3. Are my boundaries solid or fluid?
4. Do I have any false boundaries in my life, and if so, where?
5. Who in my life hates boundaries, and why did I let him/her in? Why do I keep that person around?
6. Who are the people who've watered Heaven's seeds in my life?
7. Who's watered hell's seeds in my life?
8. How important is my deliverance to me? Why or why not?
9. If I drew boundaries in every area of my life and solidified those boundaries, who would walk out of my life? Am I willing to lose those people?

10. How high are my walls (boundaries) or how low are my standards (allowances)?
11. How much has my lack of solid boundaries cost me, and am I willing to continue paying that same price over and over again for the rest of my life?
12. Do I want my parents' results, and if not, what am I doing to ensure that I don't get them?

Steps to Establishing Solid Boundaries (As Established in the Word)

Instructions	Scriptural Text	Book/Verse
Be mindful of the company you keep	Be ye not unequally yoked together with unbelievers: for what fellowship hath righteousness with unrighteousness? And what communion hath light with darkness?	2 Corinthians 6:14
Chase God, and everything else will chase you. Put God first in all things!	But seek ye first the kingdom of God, and his righteousness; and all these things shall be added unto you.	Matthew 6:33
Your body belongs to God. Deny the	I beseech you therefore, brethren, by the mercies of God, that ye present your	Romans 12:1

Instructions	Scriptural Text	Book/Verse
lusts of your flesh so that God can use your body for His glory.	bodies a living sacrifice, holy, acceptable unto God, which is your reasonable service.	
Be patient and pray.	Do not be anxious about anything, but in every situation, by prayer and petition, with thanksgiving, present your requests to God.	**Philippians 4:6 (NIV)**
Do not have any idols.	Thou shalt have no other gods before me.	**Exodus 20:3**
Remember who you belong to!	What? Know ye not that your body is the temple of the Holy Ghost which is in you, which ye have of God, and ye are not your own?	**1 Corinthians 6:19**
Do not pledge yourself to another human being; that is, until you exchange vows in marriage. Also, don't	But above all things, my brethren, swear not, neither by heaven, neither by the earth, neither by any other oath: but let your yea be yea; and your nay, nay; lest ye fall into condemnation.	**James 5:12**

Instructions	Scriptural Text	Book/Verse
make promises.		
Self explanatory!	Flee fornication. Every sin that a man doeth is without the body; but he that committeth fornication sinneth against his own body.	1 Corinthians 6:18
Do not engage in sexual immorality or any idolatrous practice.	For this is the will of God, even your sanctification, that ye should abstain from fornication: That every one of you should know how to possess his vessel in sanctification and honour; Not in the lust of concupiscence, even as the Gentiles which know not God: That no man go beyond and defraud his brother in any matter: because that the Lord is the avenger of all such, as we also have forewarned you and testified. For God hath not called us unto uncleanness, but unto	1 Thessalonians 4:3-7

Instructions	Scriptural Text	Book/Verse
	holiness.	
Avoid narcissistic people; yes, even the religious ones!	For men shall be lovers of their own selves, covetous, boasters, proud, blasphemers, disobedient to parents, unthankful, unholy, Without natural affection, trucebreakers, false accusers, incontinent, fierce, despisers of those that are good, traitors, heady, highminded, lovers of pleasures more than lovers of God; having a form of godliness, but denying the power thereof: from such turn away.	2 Timothy 3:2-5

Boundaries sometimes look and feel like obstacles, keeping us from getting what we want in the time frame that we think we need it. But many of us have learned the hard way why God established boundaries around us, just as He established boundaries around the waters and every system He created. Everything that's valuable to God, He placed a boundary around it. But because we have "will" and the freedom to exercise that will, we have all gone astray, looking for love, acceptance and affirmation, only to find ourselves being pummeled by life. We all have potential; we all have seeds in us that were planted by God and seeds that were planted by the enemy. If we stay in the will of God, Satan has no opportunity to water the seeds he's planted, but if we allow our fantasies and lusts to lead us astray, we'll find ourselves in the wilderness, trying to tame every wild animal that dares to approach us. Take inventory of your life and start drawing boundaries. Remember, some of the people in your life will exit the minute you draw and consistently enforce these boundaries, but also remember that when they leave, they provide God with the space to send the right people and lead you to where He's called you to be. You got this because God's got you!

BOUNDARIES: THE PAIN AND THE PROMISE

If you were to hang a picture on the wall and you balanced that picture on both sides to make it perfectly even, it would still look crooked, depending on the angle in which you view it. If you stood slightly to the left of the picture, it would look as if it were slightly tilted to the left; if you stood to the right of the picture, it would look like it was slightly tilted to the right. But if you stood directly in front of the picture, it would look balanced; that is, if you don't tilt your head. Straight lines oftentimes appear to be crooked to a person who's viewing them from a wrong perspective. For example, God is holy; there is no sin in Him. He cannot tell a lie, nor can He be tempted with evil. He is good everyday and forevermore. Nevertheless, many people feel like He's relatively good, but they don't realize that He's perfect in all His ways. Some people don't think He's good at all because of their experiences with people. This simply means that these individuals are not aligned with God's vision for their lives. Consequently, from where they stand, He appears to be slightly off-center, so they spend quite a bit of time trying to adjust His perspective, instead of their own. This causes them to trust in their own devices or, better yet, it causes them to lean to their own understanding. It goes without saying that when this happens, they end up attracting a bunch of broken, twisted and crooked people who appear to be right or righteous because of where they're standing. They then invite these people into the most sacred part of themselves, which is their hearts. The person enters their lives and wreaks havoc, destroying every bit of self-esteem that they have. This further perverts their perception of God because the more twisted your perspective is, the more unjust or unfair God will appear to you. To readjust your perspective, you would have to remove the profane, unholy or, better yet, ungodly people from your sacred place. After this, you'd likely need therapy and deliverance. All the same, you'd need to study the Word, and not just study, but apply the Word in every area of your life. Eventually, your perspective of God would shift until you find yourself fully aligned with His heart and will for you.

As you can probably tell by now, I teach heavily on the topic of accountability. One reason for this is—most people are surface-thinkers, meaning, they focus on what manifests above the surface, all the while, ignoring the seeds beneath the surface that yielded them the harvests that they are now complaining about. I teach a lot online (especially YouTube) about the importance of taking control of your life, but first, I help people to see the wrong turns they've made; this allows them to better understand why they've reached the places and the conclusions that they've arrived at. This also helps them to turn their lives back around; this way, they can finally start reaping the fruits that they want to see in their lives. One lesson I often teach people is this—someone could rape another human being, torment that person for years on end, and do some pretty wicked things to just about every person he or she encounters, and that person could still end up spending eternity in Heaven if he or she truly and wholeheartedly repents. However, one of that person's victims could be a law-abiding citizen who gets married, never rapes or hurts anyone and that person could frequent church regularly and still end up spending eternity in hell if he or she doesn't forgive the person or the people who hurt the individual. It seems unfair using our human perspective, but we have to remember that God is not human; His thoughts are above our thoughts and His ways are above our ways. In other words, He truly sees the bigger picture because He is God! Our human logic cannot, does not and will never be sound enough to fully understand Him. This is why we have to stop humanizing Him. To humanize God means to look at Him from the wrong angle. Again, when we do this, God could easily appear to be crooked when, in truth, He is righteous, perfect and without sin.

First and foremost, how could a wicked rapist and murderer end up in Heaven? It's simple. By truly repenting, the guy is no longer wicked. He's no longer a rapist, nor is he a murderer. Remember that Christ carried his sins to the cross, and if he TRULY repents, he will be a different creature, meaning he'll see life and people differently. All the same, he'd be regretful and remorseful for the wrongs he's done. If this upsets you, it's because you've humanized God and you think that He can be manipulated. He's our Creator! We couldn't manipulate Him if we tried everyday! What this means is that no man or woman can offer God false repentance and get away with it. God looks at the heart of a man, and the way He determines whether or not that person is being truthful is by pairing up what's in that man's heart with the words that are coming out of his mouth. If they don't align, the man is a liar. If his heart says, "Those people deserved everything that happened to them, but because I don't want to go to hell, let me go down to the altar at church and repent," he didn't truly repent! Remember, God saw what was in Lucifer's heart, even though he said contrary to what he thought. In other words, no manipulators will slither into Heaven! So, if the former rapist and murderer truly repents and God hears his heart repenting along with his lips, and of course, if he has received Jesus Christ as his Lord and Savior, God will forgive him. After all, this is why Jesus went to the cross! Consider all the sins that King David committed. He slept with Uriah's wife and had Uriah placed on the front line of a war so that he could be killed. Additionally, he rebelled against God and counted Israel; consequently, seventy thousand Israelites died as a result of David's sin. These are just a couple of the wrong turns that David made, and get this—people were hurt as a result of David's choices! Nevertheless, God still referred to him as a man after His own heart. Why? Because David truly repented! The person who was raped would have the responsibility of forgiving the rapist; this doesn't mean that the rapist will never pay for his crimes against her (don't focus on the gender; this is just an example). It simply means that she is releasing the guy to be judged by the Most

High God. This allows God to truly heal and deliver her, and this also allows God to give her insight, revelation and wisdom regarding what she's endured. Because of this, she could then help educate and heal other women and men who've been raped, and she can help prevent others from getting raped. You see, God doesn't want us living as victims because we then become powerless to help ourselves and others, but whenever we overcome what the enemy has done to us, we can be the Moses who the Lord uses to set His people free; we can be the Harriet Tubmans that He uses to lead His people to freedom. Moses escaped to Midian for forty years before he was able to go back and free others. Harriet Tubman escaped to the North before she returned to the South to set others free. The point is, you must free yourself before you can help others, otherwise, you'd spend the rest of your life being a victim. Why is this bad? It keeps you outside of your purpose, for one. And also, the food chain dictates that prey naturally, instinctively and consistently attract predators. A man or a woman who thinks and lives as prey will consistently and repeatedly attract predatory people. And before you think that I've lived an easy life, let me share with you an overview of what my life has been like.

I've seen the worst sides of the best people. Let me explain. I was born in Greenville, Mississippi in 1977 to a poor African American father and a poor African American mother. Thankfully, my parents were married, however, they weren't the least bit happy with one another. All the same, I was brought up in a very dysfunctional home. I suffered through just about every sin and crime that a young lady could suffer through growing up as a poor African American girl in one of the poorest states in America, including rape and molestation. Sexual perversion was commonplace in my family, plus, my parents had absolutely no boundaries as it relates to who they let in their home. So, my childhood was every bit of traumatic. I suffered through my first brutal rape at the age of ten-years old. I was raped by a 13-year old neighbor of ours. Not knowing how to navigate through such an event, my mother chose to whoop me. Again, she wasn't bad; she genuinely didn't know any better. She was simply repeating what had been done to her. The odds were stacked against me. I've experienced or been on the receiving end of just about every major "ism" in the book, from racism to classism to sexism. I say this to say that I was considered the scum of the Earth. Most people didn't see me as a little girl with a bright future; they saw a statistic in the making. I was a little girl growing up in the ghetto to a working mother and a father who couldn't keep a job. Additionally, my parents fought often, so it was not unusual to see the cops at our house. I was a little girl who benefited from public aid. For a while, I doubt if Satan even saw me as a threat. Howbeit, I soon learned that the hardest fight that I would have to endure would be fighting to get past all of the opinions, isms and negative expectations that people so freely attached to me. You see, when you come from the bottom, people don't mind showing you their true selves. This is why I said I've seen the worst sides of the best people. And I also learned that these can be the most dangerous people because after they're done mishandling, judging and mistreating you, they expect you to remain in the slums of life. They literally have no good expectations of you as a human. This is what makes them dangerous! For example, consider the Rosewood Massacre that took place in 1923. Let's briefly review that story. The following article was taken from Wikipedia.

Rosewood, Florida

"The initial settlers of Rosewood were both black and white. When most of the cedar trees in the area had been cut by 1890, the pencil mills closed, and many white residents moved to Sumner. By 1900, the population in Rosewood had become predominantly black. The village of Sumner was predominantly white, and relations between the two communities were relatively amicable. The population of Rosewood peaked in 1915 at 355 people.

Two black families in Rosewood named Goins and Carrier were the most influential. The Goins family brought the turpentine industry to the area, and in the years preceding the attacks, were the second largest landowners in Levy County. To avoid lawsuits from white competitors, the Goins brothers moved to Gainesville, and the population of Rosewood decreased slightly. The Carriers were also a large family, responsible for logging in the region. By the 1920s, almost everyone in the close-knit community was distantly related to each other. Although residents of Rosewood probably did not vote because voter registration requirements in Florida had effectively disfranchised blacks since the turn of the century, both Sumner and Rosewood were part of a single voting precinct counted by the U.S. Census. In 1920, the combined population of both towns was 344 blacks and 294 whites.

Before the Massacre

As was common in the late 19th century South, Florida had imposed legal racial segregation under Jim Crow laws, requiring separate black and white public facilities and transportation. Blacks and whites created their own community centers: in 1920, **the residents of Rosewood were mostly self-sufficient**. They had three churches, a school, a large Masonic Hall, a turpentine mill, a sugarcane mill, a baseball team named the Rosewood Stars, and two general stores, one of which was white-owned. The village had about a dozen two-story wooden plank homes, other small two-room houses, and several small unoccupied plank farm and storage structures. Some families owned pianos, organs, and other symbols of middle-class prosperity. Survivors of the Rosewood Massacre remember it as a happy place.

Rosewood Massacre

In January 1923, white men from nearby towns lynched a Rosewood resident allegedly in response to a lie that a white woman in nearby Sumner had been beaten and possibly raped by a black drifter. The woman was actually beaten up by her lover while her husband was at work. When black citizens defended themselves against further attack, several hundred whites organized to comb the countryside hunting for black people and burned almost every structure in Rosewood. Survivors hid for several days in nearby swamps and were evacuated by train and car to larger towns. Although state and local authorities were aware of the violence, they made no arrests for the activities in Rosewood. The town was abandoned by black residents during the attacks. None ever returned."

Source: Wikipedia/Rosewood, Florida

If you believe for one moment that this massacre was in direct response to a woman claiming to have been raped, you clearly don't know the history of racism in America. The woman's lies initiated the attack, but this attack was mainly backed by how the attackers saw Black men and women. You see, whenever people see you as a nobody and they attempt to enforce their views of you by segregating or separating themselves from you, they've sentenced you to a life of nothingness. From there, they forget about you because they've pretty much filed you away as a nobody and they don't expect to hear from you again; that is, unless you commit a crime or do something that they feel that you're prone to doing. This is the history of the human race! However, whenever you don't fit into the shoe boxes that they designed for you, but instead, you escape it, build systems and begin to thrive, those same people will look for ways to bring you back in subjection to their ideologies of you or they'll try to destroy you. This isn't just an issue of racism, we see this in classism as well. Anytime the oppressed thrive underneath the thumbs of their oppressors, the oppressors will often respond by increasing the pressure. We see this in the story of the Israelites versus the wicked Pharaoh. Let's look at that story.

Exodus 1:8-16: Now there arose a new king over Egypt, who did not know Joseph. And he said to his people, "Behold, the people of Israel are too many and too mighty for us. Come, let us deal shrewdly with them, lest they multiply, and, if war breaks out, they join our enemies and fight against us and escape from the land." Therefore they set taskmasters over them to afflict them with heavy burdens. They built for Pharaoh store cities, Pithom and Raamses. But the more they were oppressed, the more they multiplied and the more they spread abroad. And the Egyptians were in dread of the people of Israel. So, they ruthlessly made the people of Israel work as slaves and made their lives bitter with hard service, in mortar and brick, and in all kinds of work in the field. In all their work they ruthlessly made them work as slaves.

Then the king of Egypt said to the Hebrew midwives, one of whom was named Shiphrah and the other Puah, "When you serve as midwife to the Hebrew women and see them on the birthstool, if it is a son, you shall kill him, but if it is a daughter, she shall live."

As you can see, this is the history of the human race! Anytime a people are oppressed and discounted, the most dangerous thing that they can do is live outside of their oppressors' restricted understanding of them. Once someone discounts you, that person has volunteered to become your oppressor. This may sound outlandish and far-fetched; that is, until you start rising above what they said or thought about you! This is when they'll spread rumors and attempt to do any and everything to keep you from rising above their opinions of you. I said all that to say that I had a lot of Goliaths to get past, nevertheless, I chose to forgive them. This is a choice that I have to make often because I soon realized that many believers are bound by isms, including the theories or beliefs behind classism as well. In other words, the minute they say in their hearts that you are a nobody and that you'll never amount of anything, they will discount you and toss you to the back of their minds. That is, until God starts raising you up. The most dangerous thing you can ever do is get your oppressors' attention. We've all heard the adage, "Out of sight, out of mind," but here's the truth—the minute an enemy hears your name attached to anything contrary to his or her will for you, that person will begin undergoing an internal war. In this war, confusion, entitlement, comparison, anger and victimhood will join forces and cast you as a villain; this is what provokes jealousy. The Bible tells us that jealousy is as cruel as the grave! This is why He said He uses the foolish things of this world to confound the wise. Many people don't realize that they are tools being used by the enemy to suppress and oppress other people; that is, until someone who they love and respect points out their narcissistic ways. In other words, you are the picture that God hung on the wall, and anyone who's view of you is crooked is someone who is not aligned with God's vision for you. In other words, that person is not called to walk with you. Howbeit, despite the many horror stories that I could bore you with, I had to take accountability for everything that happened to the adult-sized me. I also had to stop romanticizing the concept of deliverance, after all, I needed a LOT of healing and deliverance. I used to think of deliverance being an event where people surrounded you, prayed for you and loved on you. Whatever demons you had would be called out and you'd live happily ever after, surrounded by loving people who you could also share your heart and love with. That's not how deliverance has looked for me. It oftentimes looked like me getting past another person's perception of who I am, who I should be or who I used to be. It looked like me being dragged out of my personal Egypt and then trying to settle down in the wilderness, only to learn that I was far away from where God had called me to. It looked like me having to heal time and time again because I'd invited the wrong people in my life, and every time I decided to grow more in the Lord, I'd have to watch these people fall away from me. I'm saying all this to say that creating boundaries is a very painful event, but it's necessary to get you to where God has called you.

Imagine Israel's dilemma. They had been in Egypt all of their lives by the time Moses came to rescue them. Egypt was all they knew; slavery was all they knew. And while Pharaoh was a wicked and cruel oppressor, they'd grown quite accustomed to being his slaves. Moses came along telling them about a world outside of the only world that they knew. He talked to them about living when all they knew how to do was survive. He talked to them about worshiping when all they knew how to do was cry. This is the dilemma many empaths and prophetic people find themselves in. They only know how to survive. This is why it is so difficult to help many people get free. Believe it or not, many prophets and prophetic people are accustomed to dealing with narcissists, so while they may complain about their individual pharaohs and even attempt to escape them a few times, they don't know any other way to live outside of being abused and oppressed. So, they often do the exact thing that the Israelites did. The Israelites followed Moses into and across the Red Sea. They followed Moses into the wilderness, but the minute they got tired, the minute they got hungry, the minute they got thirsty or, better yet, the minute their flesh wasn't satisfied, they started fantasizing about Egypt again. If they could have, many of them would have dragged Pharaoh's lifeless body from the sea, performed CPR on him and propped him back up on his throne. They'd then go back to the bondage that they were accustomed to and chuckle whenever Pharaoh's henchmen came out onto the yard to harass and humiliate them. They'd lie to themselves all over again, choosing to believe that under all of Pharaoh's heartlessness, he had managed to find some way to love and appreciate them. After all, isn't this what we tell ourselves about broken, toxic and narcissistic people? Underneath it all, they truly love us—they just don't know how to express it. This is a lie from the pit of hell! God is love. In other words, love is not an emotion; love is a Spirit. Love is the expression of who God is. Love is not abusive, nor is it condescending. Love does not lead anyone into sin, but away from it. This is why you can't get angry with someone who claimed to have loved you, only for that person to show you otherwise. For example, if you were dating a man and he adamantly claimed to love you, but in the end, he abused, betrayed and abandoned you, please note that he didn't necessarily deceive you, not intentionally anyhow. In most cases, he himself was deceived. You see, he likely never experienced true love, and like most people today, he thought love was an emotion. He settled for Hollywood's depiction of love, which is nothing more than oxytocin-driven lust triggered by words, music and sex. In other words, he was under the influence. He eventually sobered up and realized that he didn't love you. He eventually fell into the generational snares that the men in his family had fallen into. You couldn't save him. As a matter of fact, as pharaonic and narcissistic as he was, if you were saved when you were dating him, you also served as his pharaoh. Remember, in the Kingdom of God, you are the predator whenever you go after an unbeliever or a new believer. In Matthew 6:8, Jesus said, "But whoso shall offend one of these little ones which believe in me, it were better for him that a millstone were hanged about his neck, and that he were drowned in the depth of the sea." In the Kingdom, you would be that guy's pharaoh because you're attempting to make him serve a God he doesn't want to serve. You're acting as a taskmaster, trying to force him to do the things that you believe would benefit your relationship with him. Read that again. But in the kingdom of darkness or, better yet, the world's system, you were the victim because you tried to do the right thing for the wrong person. This would make him your pharaoh in that system, and consequently, many worldly women would surround and attempt to comfort you. They'd tell you about their philandering, pharaonic and narcissistic lovers or past lovers as well. If you want something from the Kingdom, you've have to wholeheartedly repent and surrender not just your life, but your gifts to God. An unsubmitted gift can and will be used, oftentimes as a token of witchcraft by the enemy. This means that you have to finally get in God's will and start drawing boundaries around yourself. This sounds easy enough, but it can be disheartening as well because true, God-established and solid boundaries will always reveal the motives, the character and the hearts of the people you've invited into your world. Many of these people will eventually decline your invitation because boundaries keep them from getting whatever it is that they want from you. Having boundaries forces everyone who chooses to remain in your life to have a balanced relationship with you, meaning, they can't take advantage of you anymore. This is what most of us want, however, when you're transitioning from pharaonic relationships to covenant relationships, the journey can be pretty lengthy and pretty painful. Consider this—many of the Israelites died in the wilderness on their way to the Promised Land. This is because they murmured and complained, instead of being grateful to God for delivering them from Pharaoh. This pattern can still be seen today. There are people out there who are literally angry with God because He delivered them from a narcissist. He allowed some woman or some man to come into the narcissist's life and distract the toxic soul; this way, He could provide a way of escape for His people. But a lot of people don't see it this way. Instead, they see God as unfair and unbalanced because, according to them, He allowed their narcissistic lovers to hurt, betray and abandon them. This goes back to the waiting room of the soul. Remember, whenever the enemy gets into the subconscious and successfully plants lies there, he will then remove as much truth from the subconscious as well. He will then harden the subconscious in an event called pride; this makes it difficult for the truth to penetrate your heart. When someone tells you the truth after you have been infested with lies, those truths go and sit in the waiting room of your soul. Many of the lies you've been told will then march forward to confront the truths; this is when a war then breaks out between the truth and the lies. This war is called confusion. If you genuinely want the truth, you'll study, ask questions and pray. This allows the truth to overcome the lies. If you don't want the truth, you'll become offended and reach out to the wrong people to aid you in the fight, or you'll just reject the truth altogether by saying things like:

- "Well, God knows my heart!"
- "Judge ye not unless (it's supposed to be lest, but I digress) ye be judged!"

- "Can we change the subject?"

This is referred to as the spirit of bondage. It is the spirit behind the slave mentality. What makes this spirit so effective is the fact that it builds a siege wall around the subconscious of its prey; again, this wall is called pride. Guarding this wall, you'll find haughty spirits, the spirits of offense, religious spirits and a host of other guarding spirits. Their assignment is to keep the truth out, all the while, ushering falsehoods in. Someone bound by these spirits will constantly make excuses for their abusers in an attempt to convince others that there is hope for their pharaohs. This is also done to enlist the aid of others in their attempts to usher their narcissistic lovers, friends or family members into the will of God. Remember this—you can't drag someone to the cross! They have to come willingly; it must be a desire that they truly possess. All the same, God must draw them. John 6:44 confirms this. It reads, "No one can come to me unless the Father who sent me draws him. And I will raise him up on the last day." Remember, in Book One, I shared my testimony of salvation. I was driving back to my hometown in the middle of the night. My closest friend at the time was in the passenger's seat of my car. We had just left a nightclub and we were both intoxicated. Somehow, I didn't realize that the street ahead was curving, so I started driving towards some trees off road. That's when my friend screamed, "Tiffany, what are you doing?!" In that moment, I realized that we were seconds away from hitting a tree. I laughed aloud at myself, and for a short period of time, we didn't say anything.

My friend then broke the silence. She said, "Tiffany, we gotta stop doing this." We then started talking about Christ and church, and she mentioned that her aunt was a member of Agape Storge Christian Center. I'd heard of the church, but didn't know too much about it. We agreed to go there that following Sunday, and three weeks later, I joined the church. Get this—God had been drawing my heart for years! And this tug on my heart had recently began to intensify and become almost irresistible, so when my friend mentioned going to church, I literally let out a sigh of relief. I think my greatest fear at that time was walking away from everything that I knew to follow Christ, but ultimately, that's what I had to do. Over the course of time, I watched people fall out of my life in droves. And the issue wasn't me being mean or religious. In truth, for nearly a decade, I wrestled with the same sins I'd walked into the church with. But every year, there had been a drastic change to my thinking and my life. One by one, I walked away from the sins I once enjoyed, and when I walked away from those issues, I lost friends and loved ones. What was I doing? I was allowing God to loosen the chains of bondage until I was finally set free. And it was a painful, yet beautiful process. I don't mention the pain to discourage anyone, but I want to give you a realistic view of the journey ahead. Then again, it may not be as painful for you as it was for me because again, I had a lot of isms to overcome. Every "ism" is a Goliath, and every Goliath must be slayed by a David. And by David, I'm not talking about a specific anointing, I'm talking about a specific stage that the prophetic individual enters when he or she matures and wakes up to his or her identity. Remember, David in the Bible served his father by working in the field. Before going up against Goliath, he had to fight a few wild animals; this is what prepared and qualified him to go up against the giant. In 1 Samuel 17:36, he told King Saul, "Your servant has struck down both lions and bears, and this uncircumcised Philistine shall be like one of them, for he has defied the armies of the living God." This means that you don't date what you come across in the wilderness, you slay it! And by slay, I don't mean that you are to kill a person. Your job is to overcome the spirit that's in that person because, in truth, that's where your real fight lies! Ephesians 6:12 (ESV) says it this way, "For we do not wrestle against flesh and blood, but against the rulers, against the authorities, against the cosmic powers over this present darkness, against the spiritual forces of evil in the heavenly places." Our fight isn't against what we see or who we see; our real fight is against Satan and his angels (demons)! You don't overcome the narcissist by breaking up with him or her; this is just the starting line of the battle. You have to divorce the spirit that's in the narcissist! How do you do this? First and foremost, you must educate yourself about:

1. The prophetic anointing.
2. The Jezebel spirit (the spirit behind narcissism).
3. The Ahab spirit (the spirit behind the broken empath).
4. Fear.
5. The Kingdom of God (above all).

Understand this—you have a purpose that you may be

unaware of, but Satan is not fully unaware of your assignment or your identity. He just wants to keep you in the dark; this way, you will pose no threat to him or his kingdom. He wants to distract and overwhelm you so that you'll spend the rest of your life entertaining the wrong people or healing from the wounds inflicted on you in those relationships. What's crazy is—most people are afraid of the pain that comes with walking away from who they want to be; they are afraid of embracing who they're designed to be. Nevertheless, they will stick around for decades and even lifetimes enduring the agony brought onto them by their narcissistic lovers or loved ones. I remember being at the edge of my sanity, broken, suicidal and terrified of what the next day would bring. Yes, I was married to a narcissist, and believe it or not, dealing with those emotions had become a norm to me. And as commonplace as they were, I could never truly adapt to the dread, the torment and the unpredictability of the beautifully decorated dungeon that we called marriage. One day, I asked myself a life-changing question. I was driving in my car, dreading going home; I was sad, anxious, fearful and desperate. My inner dialogue went like this:

"Tiffany, why won't you leave?"

"Because I'm scared of the pain of being without him."

"Aren't you already in pain?!"

"Yeah, but we do have some good days."

"Okay, consider this—if you leave, you'll definitely go through the pain associated with a breakup, but on average, that pain should subside in six to twelve months. If you stay, you'll be in pain for the rest of your life which, of course, will be short-lived if you stay."

I then imagined my funeral. The lies that the enemy once told me began to evaporate. At one point, I used to literally fantasize of dying. This is common for prophetic people! I'm sharing this raw testimony to help you understand that those crazy thoughts that you have are every bit of demonic! I used to fantasize about my then husband coming to my funeral and crying at the top of his lungs. I imagined a bunch of guys holding him back while he repeatedly shouted, "Baby, I'm sorry!" In that moment, he would finally get it. He'd finally understand that I was a good woman all along, and he would finally understand just how much pain he'd inflicted on my heart. But that day in my car, the veil came off that lie. I suddenly realized that this was NOT at all how my funeral would be had I stayed with him. Would he have shed a few tears? Absolutely! But would they be driven by grief? Nope. It would have presented a moment for him to get the attention and the sympathy of everyone around him. He would then leave that funeral and go be with one of his girlfriends who would then "comfort" him while I rotted. Those thoughts absolutely changed the way that I saw our relationship. I came to realize that I didn't possess the tools to fix the cracks in his broken soul. All the same, I needed some soul-work done on myself—obviously! So, I made up my mind that I was going to have to take a right turn. I was also honest with myself. I told myself that it was going to hurt, and it was going to hurt bad! I told myself that I was going to need help from some loved ones to get through that pain! I told myself that I needed to make sure that I only enlisted the help of people who pushed me forward, and not people who held me back by monitoring my soon-to-be ex or constantly bringing his name up. I told myself that I needed some tough love! I'm sharing this story so you'll understand that the promises of God are available for you, but it doesn't come without pain. But get this—the pain is bearable; it's the fear and the anticipation of the pain that brings us the most torment. For example, if your parents used corporal punishment to discipline you when you were a child, you can likely attest to this—if your mother or father said, "I'm going to whoop you when you get home," the whooping itself was bad, but the most agonizing and tormenting part was the anticipation of the whooping. It was walking alongside that parent, knowing that whenever you got home, you were going to get a spanking. The same is true whenever you consider walking away from broken and toxic people. The fear of being alone is far worse than the actual event itself! For example, the Israelites started fantasizing about Egypt again because they couldn't conceptualize what the Promised Land would look like. The spirit of bondage had them so entangled in its chains that they actually desired to go back to the land and the situation that God had delivered them from! The spirit of bondage is the same spirit that makes a heroin addict miss living in the slums and killing himself with drugs! The spirit of bondage is the same spirit that would convince a woman to go to court and defend a man who kidnapped and raped her repeatedly; they call this Stockholm's Syndrome, but it's just the spirit of bondage! The spirit of bondage is the same demon that will make a man or a woman walk away from an amazing marriage to pursue a person who has little to no morals. It's a spirit! And get this—spirits don't come out just because you point them out. True deliverance comes through education! This is why every empath/prophetic individual should pray and ask the Lord to lead them into a prophetic community; this way, they can come to understand just how they are wired and why they are here! Without this knowledge, the enemy will continue to hijack their minds and their lives; that is, until they have been consumed by pain. In the year 2018, the CDC's National Center for Health Statistics recorded 48,344 suicides and 1.4 million suicide attempts that took place in the United States alone! In truth, the majority of these people were likely prophetic! 1 Kings 18:3-6 reads, "And Ahab called Obadiah, which was the governor of his house. (Now Obadiah feared the LORD greatly: <u>For it was so, when Jezebel cut off the prophets of the LORD</u>, that Obadiah took an hundred prophets, and hid them by fifty in a cave, and fed them with bread and water.) And Ahab said unto Obadiah, Go into the land, unto all fountains of water, and unto all brooks: peradventure we may find grass to save the horses and mules alive, that we lose not all the beasts. So they divided the land between them to pass throughout it: Ahab went one way by himself, and Obadiah went another way by himself." Remember, the Jezebel spirit is the classic narcissist; it's the spirit behind narcissism, Narcissistic

Personality Disorder and Borderline Personality Disorder! This is just a short list! And as you can see, that spirit has been obsessed with destroying prophets and prophetic individuals for thousands of years! This is to say that you're not the first empath to deal with the narcissist and you definitely won't be the last; that is, unless the world comes to a screeching halt today. But the Promised Land that God has waiting for you is more than worth the pain and the journey. Please note that by Promised Land, I'm not talking about Heaven; we'll get there when it's our time. I'm talking about the promises of God that are waiting for you to grow up in the Lord so that you can pull them down. And it's okay if you can't imagine a life outside of what you know. This is normal. I didn't leave Mississippi until I was 29-years old. Before then, I'd only traveled to neighboring states of Arkansas, Tennessee and Louisiana. I'd also traveled to Milwaukee, Wisconsin when I was 14 and again when I was 15-years old, and from there, I'd visited Muskegon, Michigan. That's all! I had never been on a plane, a ship or a train before then. My world was absolutely tiny! But I started traveling and this absolutely changed my life and my mind!

How do you divorce the spirit of bondage once and for all?

1. **Educate yourself!** Below, I've listed a few books that every prophet and prophetic individual should invest in. Also, get yourself a mentor. Ask the Lord to point you in the direction of a mentor, and be sure to commit to (1) not quitting and (2) investing in yourself. Note: you'll have to pull the siege wall down that's

surrounding your heart (if you have one). This wall is the wall of pride. The only way to receive new revelation is you'll have to allow the truth to get past the waiting room of your conscious. Pray and ask the Lord to give you a heart of flesh (see Ezekiel 36:26).

2. **Get into a prophetic community.** I'm not telling you to leave your church, but it is a good idea to look for a prophetic community that you can visit and glean from. Or, at minimum, go to some prophetic conferences whenever they come to your neck of the woods.

3. **Take accountability for what happened to the adult-sized you.** Blame is the accent of the bound. Accountability is the language of freedom.

4. **Go through deliverance!** Look up some deliverance ministries or conferences in your area. Note: most deliverance ministries embrace the prophetic.

5. **Don't date until you're healed and mature.** This involves accountability. Be accountable to your pastor or mentor regarding your love life.

6. **Volunteer at your church.** I advise people to do this because most empaths have the gift of charity. They need to give something somewhere because if they don't, they'll relieve themselves by giving to the narcissist!

7. **Get counseling.** I can't emphasize this enough! Find a therapist and schedule some appointments to start your healing journey!

8. **Surround yourself with emotionally and spiritually**

healthy people. This may take time because we attract what we are, so get the healing and deliverance you'll need to attract the right types of people in your life.

9. **Change your phone number.** The people from your past should not have access to you, especially when you're healing.

10. **Write the vision and make it plain.** Write down what you want for yourself, and then list the boundaries you'll need to protect every one of those structures. Create your boundaries, publish your boundaries and enforce your boundaries. If someone walks out of your life because of your boundaries, please note that your boundaries are doing what they are designed to do—protect you from lawless people. This is so that you can build healthy functioning systems in your life—systems that produce peace and prosperity!

11. **Stop fantasizing about Egypt.** On your journey to the promise, you will go through several wilderness seasons. Don't date or court while you're there and don't allow impatience, frustration or loneliness to cause you to start romanticizing Egypt again. Move forward, not backwards! Remember, whatever you focus your attention on, your legs will slowly begin to follow. Sometimes, you have to give yourself a gentle or not-so-gentle tug (reminder) of the pain you endured in Egypt.

12. **Align your heart with God's heart.** Remember, this is what you need to clearly see the picture that God

painted for you!

Remember, true deliverance can be uncomfortable, and in many cases, it can be painful, but it produces beauty in the end! Every person who has taken and completed this journey can attest to this fact—God's plans for you will absolutely blow your mind in the end! He'll give you peace on every side, He'll surround you with love and He'll eventually use you to help free others, including many of your loved ones. He'll change how you see Him, and whenever you are aligned with His Word, He'll change how you see yourself! Remind yourself everyday that God loves you. Just saying this alone is sometimes powerful enough to dislodge and chase away the spirit of bondage. Below, I've listed several books that you should invest in so that you can grow into the man or the woman God designed, called and/or chose you to be! Please note that these are just book suggestions. You can conduct your own research by asking around and reading Amazon reviews. All the same, you don't have to purchase the books mentioned; they are suggestions. If you prefer, you can purchase them one at a time. This is all up to you!

Book Suggestions	
The Prophet's Manual John Eckhardt	**Prophetic Science** (series) Bryan Meadows
Prophet Arise John Eckhardt	**The Cave** Bryan Meadows
Destroying the Spirit of	**How to Study the Bible**

Rejection John Eckhardt	Bryan Meadows
Discerning and Defeating the Ahab Spirit: The Key to Breaking Free from Jezebel Steve Sampson	**Hell's Toxic Trio: Defeat the Demonic Spirits that Stall Your Destiny** Ryan Lestrange
Kingdom Authority: Taking Dominion Over the Powers of Darkness Kynan Bridges	**Supernaturally Delivered: A Practical Guide to Deliverance and Spiritual Warfare** John Veal
The Power of Prophetic Prayer: Release Your Destiny Kynan Bridges	**Rethinking Narcissism: The Secret to Recognizing and Coping with Narcissists** Dr. Craig Malkin
Breaking the Power of Familiar Spirits: How to Deal with Demonic Conspiracies Kimberly Daniels	**The Secrets to Deliverance: Defeat the Toughest Cases of Demonic Bondage** Alexander Pagani
Fasting for Breakthrough and Deliverance John Eckhardt	**Jezebellion** (series) Tiffany Buckner

These are just a few suggestions. Be sure to ask around and look at reviews as well. And of course, be sure to move on to

Book Three of the Boundaries series, where you'll continue to learn more about boundaries and boundary types!

A Note to the Empath and the Prophetic Individual

First and foremost, let's address the term "empath." Of course, it comes from the word "empathy," which is defined by Merriam Webster as "the action of understanding, being aware of, being sensitive to, and vicariously experiencing the feelings, thoughts, and experience of another of either the past or present without having the feelings, thoughts, and experience fully communicated in an objectively explicit manner." The word "empath" was first used in science fiction in 1956 and gained a small measure of traction in 1968 when it was modeled on the hit show Star Trek. As the worldwide internet began to gain momentum, more awareness was brought to this term, and it was eventually adopted by the medical world to describe people who had a natural inclination to experience the emotions of others. But what's even more amazing is that God described empathy in the Bible. We simply didn't identify the term because it was hidden behind our interpretation of 1 Corinthians 13:2, which reads "And though I have the gift of prophecy, and understand all mysteries, and all knowledge; and though I have all faith, so that I could remove mountains, and have not charity, I am nothing." The gift of charity is also mentioned in 1 Corinthians 13:13, which reads "And now abideth faith, hope, charity, these three; but the greatest of these is charity" and 1 Corinthians 14:1, which reads,

"Follow after charity, and desire spiritual gifts, but rather that ye may prophesy." In modern translations, the word "charity" was replaced with the word "love," and while this isn't an inaccurate translation, it is not a complete or descriptive one either. It is from where we get the word "charisma," which is defined by Bible Hub as "a gift of grace, a free gift." In Christian terminology, the word "charity" is synonymous with the word "agape," which means "the highest form of love" or "unconditional love." It also means "God's kind of love."

So, what then is the gift of charity? It is the supernatural gift and ability to love others beyond the human expression. It is undeserved love or, better yet, a love that provokes us to give (time, material things, ourselves) to another person or thing; it is experiencing the compassion of Christ. So, charity is love; again, the translation of the word in the modern biblical sense (translation) is not inaccurate. It's just unfinished. It is a supernatural ability; it is a gift, and it is the gift (or curse) that empaths or, better yet, prophetic people have. Again, an empath is a prophetic person; it's just the secular term for prophetic. And yes, you can be unsaved and still have, experience and tap into this ability. Romans 11:29 proves this; it reads, 'For the gifts and calling of God *are* without repentance." Howbeit, an unsaved person is not necessarily going to hear from God (in most cases); instead, an unsaved person, like a saved person, is wired to be sensitive to the presence and the voice of God, but because he or she has not confessed Jesus Christ as his or her Lord and Savior, that person's supernatural abilities can be and oftentimes is hijacked by the enemy. But what does this look like? It looks like empathy; it looks like a super loving and sensitive person surrounding himself or herself with personal projects. Of course, these projects are people who need love. Empaths or prophetic people are gifts, but when they aren't saved or don't understand their gifting, they give themselves away to the wrong people. Eventually, this causes them to despise and even attempt to reject their gifting. How do I know this? Remember, earlier in this book, I told you that my mother died from a lack of boundaries. My mother was an empath and she passed that gift on to her children. But because she didn't understand her wiring, and she didn't go to churches that could help her better understand her gift or its purpose, she kept attracting narcissists into her life. I watched them devour her time, her peace, and everything she valued, even a job she'd had for 16 years. And for this reason, I despised my gift of charity. I wanted ABSOLUTELY NOTHING to do with it because a God-given gift can and does feel like a burden and a curse when it is not explained, tamed or guarded, especially if and when the enemy hijacks it. So, what happens to a person who has the gift of charity, but quenches that overwhelming desire to give? Our gift is then perverted and again, it begins to go in reverse. In other words, we become hoarders. Along with makeup, shoes and perfume, I also hoarded my gifts and abilities. I wouldn't share them with anyone out of fear of attracting the narcissist. Obviously, I'd dealt with my fair share of narcissists, which again is the Jezebel spirit. You see, an unsaved or untrained empath will almost always find themselves bound by what we call (in the Christian realm) the Ahab spirit. If you study the biblical character Ahab, you will know that:

1. He was the king of Israel.
2. God had given the Israelites the charge or commandment to not intermarry with any of the pagan nations that surrounded them, but Ahab disobeyed God and married Jezebel. Jezebel was a Phoenician princess who worshiped the deity, Baal.
3. Ahab's marriage to Jezebel was a political move. In those days, whenever a nation was considered a super-power, meaning, it had defeated other powerful nations and was thriving, some of the weaker nations would ally with the stronger ones in order to get protection and provision from that nation. God had always fought for Israel, so they didn't need to ally themselves with anyone, nevertheless, Ahab's fear and ambition led him to do the unthinkable. He partnered up with Ithbaal (Jezebel's father/the king of Tyre), and as a sign of good faith, he'd married Ithbaal's daughter, Jezebel. Because Ahab presented Israel as the "weaker nation," this meant that Israel would become a subjugate of the pagan king. This illegal act also meant that YAHWEH would be dethroned as Israel's God, and replaced with Ithbaal's god, Baal.
4. Jezebel became queen of Israel through her marriage to Ahab, and she used her power and influence to establish (and enforce) the worship of Baal amongst

God's people. She even killed off most of God's prophets, replacing them with the prophets of Baal.

5. God kept speaking to Ahab through the prophets. He sent Elijah to rebuke Ahab a few times, and He sent Micaiah, but Ahab was a rebellious, fearful and ambitious man who didn't trust YAHWEH to protect or provide for him. So, he'd repent, but this was always short-lived.

6. God eventually used the very thing that Ahab trusted in to end his life so that He could dethrone him and replace him with someone better. The false prophets of Baal gave Ahab the clearance to go into war against Ramoth-Gilead, promising him a victory over his enemies. Instead, Ahab died in that war.

7. After Ahab died, Jezebel remained queen for another ten years. In this time, God was literally giving her the space to repent, but she did not. Eventually, God sent Jehu to her castle to dethrone and destroy her.

What I've learned about people who have the Ahab spirit is:

1. They are prophetic people who clearly have the gift of empathy.

2. They are fearful people who have likely experienced some measure of trauma in their lives, so they surround themselves with people who have the strengths that they either don't have or are afraid to tap into. In this lineup of characters, you will find narcissistic (Jezebelic) people who give the empath a false sense of security.

3. They are more at fault than the narcissist for what takes place in their lives.
4. They hate certain responsibilities, which is why they employ the help of the narcissist.

Empaths have an insatiable need to give; narcissists have an insatiable need to take. God wired empaths this way so that He could use them as the prophets and/or prophetic people He's wired them to be. Please note that not every empath is a prophet; most are prophetic, meaning, they are wired to feel, not just the presence of God, but the heart of God. This supernatural sensitivity is what we call empathy. Satan will always hijack this gift if it is not guarded by the Spirit of God. In other words, if the person who has the gift is unsaved, that gift isn't guarded—OR if the person is saved, but is not guarding his or her heart like the Bible tells us to—or if the person is operating in fear, he or she will attract the narcissist also known as the Jezebel spirit. The Jezebel spirit is attracted to the scent of untapped power and authority. If you are too afraid to touch, use or exercise your God-given authority, the Jezebel spirit will attach itself to you through a person, and began to exercise that power on your behalf. In exchange, the person harboring that spirit will offer you provision, protection and/or a sense of belonging in exchange for your voice, your time, your body and/or your material wealth. So, the relationship between the empath and the narcissist or, better yet, the Jezebel spirit and the Ahab spirit is centered wholly around codependency. A mother who has the Jezebel spirit, for example, will go out of her way to create an illegal soul tie between herself and her children. Mothers naturally have soul ties with their children, but a narcissistic mother will create or attempt to create an idolatrous appetite within her children, forcing them to crave and hunger for her love, attention and affirmation. She will hold her approval over their heads, constantly taking it from them anytime they disappoint her or anytime she feels the need to remind them of her power. She will make them financially, emotionally, psychologically, physically or socially dependent on her. She'll do this using a series of traumas from verbal abuse, physical abuse and financial abuse. I've seen many cases where mothers like these intentionally did not equip their children in the financial arena, so the children were financially handicapped. Whenever they moved out of their mothers' homes, they still reasoned like 16-year old children (as it relates to their finances), so they rarely paid their bills on time, they kept getting fired from (or quitting) their jobs and evicted from their homes. They'd always end up right back under their narcissistic mothers' controlling thumbs, even though many of them complained about her selfish, combative and narcissistic ways. I've counseled the Ahab'ed empath and I've counseled the narcissistic lover in his or her life, and I soon learned that we (the church) had it all wrong. We'd been trying to protect the empath from the narcissist, and we've taught the empath that he or she is the victim, and the narcissist is the predator, and while this has some ring of truth to it, it is not the way God sees it! Remember, Ahab in the Bible was given a gift. He was the king of Israel (legally). He was given power, authority, and most of all, God's trust. He violated them all. And while Jezebel was the assassin, the aggravator and the instigator of all the evil we witnessed during their reign, she was operating under Ahab's authority. Read that again. If Ahab had not married her and made her queen over God's people, she wouldn't have the power to inflict the evil that she'd done. All the same, Ahab had plenty of opportunities to repent, but his alliance to Ithbaal meant more to him than his alliance with God. This is why, to God, they are oftentimes more at fault than the narcissist. The narcissist simply came along because he or she was invited in to reign, rule or operate in an area that the empath was too afraid, too ambitious or too entitled to rule in. Again, an opportunist is powerless if he or she is not given an opportunity.

I've counseled empaths through some of their rawest emotions, but I had to be honest with them so that they could embrace true freedom. I've counseled empaths through everything, including the times when they passionately wanted to take their own lives or the lives of their narcissistic lovers, and I'll share with you what I've shared with them. If you murder the narcissist, you still won't be free! It's a spirit; you can't kill a demon! You can't even truly break up with a narcissist without first divorcing that spirit! This is why you keep attracting narcissistic people to you! That devil will keep coming after you until you:

1. Learn and embrace your God-given identity.
2. Learn and embrace your God-given abilities (after salvation).

3. Learn and embrace your God-given authority.

All the same, you have to be willing to lose whatever benefits you believe you are getting from the narcissist, even if that benefit is just you not having to be alone. And for the empaths who've expressed a desire to kill themselves, I say this—"Why not just lose your life for Christ?! Why not just sacrifice your desires, your plans and your comfort to live for God?" This is true sacrifice! Your desire to shed your own blood is a demonic appetite; it's Satan trying to get you to present yourself as an offering to him! Why not just go for broke and surrender wholeheartedly to God, and commit to fight against what you once empowered?

Why am I sharing this? It's to get you, the empath, the prophet or the prophetic person to understand that God entrusted you with those abilities; He gave that power to you! This means that you have to confront and defeat fear, even if that means doing everything from paying your bills to facing your enemies afraid! One of the strengths I took from my mother is the ability to endure; that is, what the Bible calls long-suffering. But I soon learned that having this gift didn't mean that I had to subject myself to the wrong people and suffer through their narcissistic tantrums or emotional flexing. I could suffer long by myself if I had to! And I did just that! I closed the door on every narcissist by simply drawing and enforcing boundaries around myself. To dismantle those boundaries, a few of my narcissistic family members would say things like, "You're mean" or "You're controlling." I don't like controlling people, so one day, I asked them to give me specific examples of times when I'd attempted to control them. I literally brought them together in a room and challenged them. They couldn't do it. Instead, they described the times when I'd said "no" to them, and they placed emphasis on the fact that my "no" was a solid boundary, meaning, I was unmovable to the point where I didn't care about what I stood to lose behind my refusal to do whatever it is they wanted me to do. You see, when I found Christ, I found myself! And I arrived at a place where I was willing to lose everybody in my life if they weren't willing to respect my boundaries, and by boundaries, I mean just being loving, peaceful and respectful; that's all! It means that they can't be toxic, controlling, manipulative and condescending towards me. Our conversations have to be healthy, and if they can't be healthy for too long, they have to be short. I placed boundaries around my home, my finances, my ears and my time! A few of my family members complained when I said, for example, that no one could fornicate in my house or bring their boyfriends or girlfriends to my house. They could only bring boyfriends/girlfriends for a visit if they were faithful to these people and planning to marry them. In other words, they couldn't bring a myriad of characters to my house over time. This is order, but to a narcissist, this is control. Why? Because I'm in control of myself, and I don't depend on anyone (but God) for anything. This is true power; this is me walking in my God-given authority! One of the most narcissistic people I've ever met in my life once told me, "You don't listen! This is why I don't like you!" This woman was an in-law, meaning, I'd married into her family. I asked her to give me an example of what she meant, and she said, "When I tell you to do something, you don't do it!" I explained to her that this was control on her part, and that she had to give people the grace to tell her no. She insisted that she wasn't controlling (and oh, but she was), so I asked for another example. She said, for example, "When I tell you that you are coming to the store with me, you say no!" Of course, I told her that you can ask me if I want to come to the store, but if I say no, I'm not being mean. I just don't want to go." I learned that controlling, narcissistic people absolutely HATE being told no in any form, shape or fashion. And get this, I'm not talking about saying "no" in an aggressive or rude way. I'm talking about just saying, "No, thank you. I really don't feel like it," and saying this in the meekest, most loving and child-like way EVER—with a smile on your face! All they hear is NO! And they hate this word so much that they magnify the sound of it anytime it's said to them. Nevertheless, you have to tell people no and face the consequences, otherwise, they'll rob you of your peace.

I said all that to say this—you are only a victim if you choose to be. The real problem isn't that narcissists are taking advantage of you, the problem is that you're allowing narcissists to take advantage of you BECAUSE you don't want to lose a benefit that you feel the narcissist is giving to you. This is why you have to completely give up those fantasies and let God paint the picture of your life, otherwise, every dream, fantasy and imagination that you have will continue to grow in value. Once Satan has nothing in you, meaning, there's nothing that you want from him, every narcissist in your life will no longer be appealing to you. When you start to value your peace over whatever it is that the narcissist is holding over your head, the narcissist will lose his/her power in your life. In layman's terms, when you give up the idol (whatever it is that you want and worship), the narcissist will lose his or her seat in your life!

Note Center

Great day to you and thank you for reading the second installation of the Book of Boundaries. I pray that the information in this book not only opened your eyes, but that it also gave you the motivation, the insight and the tools you need to set and secure boundaries in your life. And since this is the second book in the series, I decided to create this section for you to document your progress as you navigate through each book and as you navigate through life in general. Use the space provided below to detail some of the lessons you've learned, how you plan to apply them and to journal about your success and failures. Happy boundary-building!

Your Name	
Today's Date	
City, State	

Who are your boundaries designed to protect?
- Name:
- Name:
- Name:
- Name:
- Name:
- Name:
- Name:
- Name:

Use this section to write a letter to the future you. Come back and read this letter anytime you need encouragement or to be reminded why you decided to set and enforce boundaries in your life.

Journal

CCLXXXIII

Printed in Great Britain
by Amazon